Father and Father

Father and Father

Witness the Divine Orchestration in an Individual's Journey

BY JENNIFER S. LEE

RESOURCE *Publications* • Eugene, Oregon

FATHER AND FATHER
Witness the Divine Orchestration in an Individual's Journey

Copyright © 2024 Jennifer S. Lee. All rights reserved. Except for brief quotations in critical publications or reviews, no part of this book may be reproduced in any manner without prior written permission from the publisher. Write: Permissions, Wipf and Stock Publishers, 199 W. 8th Ave., Suite 3, Eugene, OR 97401.

Resource Publications
An Imprint of Wipf and Stock Publishers
199 W. 8th Ave., Suite 3
Eugene, OR 97401

www.wipfandstock.com

PAPERBACK ISBN: 979-8-3852-1100-5
HARDCOVER ISBN: 979-8-3852-1101-2
EBOOK ISBN: 979-8-3852-1102-9

04/23/24

Scripture quotations marked NIV are from The Holy Bible, New International Version®, NIV® Copyright © 1973, 1978, 1984, 2011 by Biblica, Inc.® Used by permission. All rights reserved worldwide.

Scripture quotations marked ESV are from The ESV® Bible (The Holy Bible, English Standard Version®), © 2001 by Crossway, a publishing ministry of Good News Publishers. Used by permission. All rights reserved.

Scripture quotations marked KJV from The Authorized (King James) Version. Rights in the Authorized Version in the United Kingdom are vested in the Crown. Reproduced by permission of the Crown's patentee, Cambridge University Press

CONTENTS

CHAPTER 1
The Letter | 1

CHAPTER 2
Lightning Strike | 12

CHAPTER 3
My Second Parents | 21

CHAPTER 4
Family Evangelism | 31

CHAPTER 5
Happy Life in Colorado | 50

CHAPTER 6
Mom into USA | 67

CHAPTER 7
Back to Hometown | 81

CHAPTER 8
New Opportunity | 96

CHAPTER 9
Fight with Liver Cancer | 106

CHAPTER 10
Holy Ground | 120

CHAPTER 11
The Angels and Satan | 126

CHAPTER 1

The Letter

JOYFUL LETTER

I wanted to earn money quickly and help my family when I graduated from middle school. Perhaps, like me, other kids of my age felt the same way at that time. So, I decided to enroll in a technical high school instead of a general high school. In my high school, I managed to rank within the top ten of my class. It was during that time that my homeroom teacher announced the top ten students and advised other students in need of assistance to study together with those students.

When I was four years of age, I mastered the basics of Korean reading, writing, and mathematics, from an early age. I have had a strong interest in learning new things. I'm so passionate about gaining knowledge that I even call myself a "knowledge enthusiast" with an almost obsessive desire to learn new things. To satisfy my curiosity, I must excel at the knowledge I want to acquire until I feel content.

When I first entered elementary school, re-learning and teaching things that I already knew became boring, and I lost interest in studying. I didn't study at all, but I kept my school grades within the middle-high level. I had decided which high school I would like to attend, and I was temporarily moved to my aunt's place in the process of waiting to go to the high school entrance ceremony, which was closer to school than my home.

While staying at my aunt's house a phone call came. It was the news that my father, who had been on a one-year contract in Saudi Arabia, would return a few months early before the contract expired. That night, I couldn't sleep due to the joy and excitement of meeting my beloved father earlier. Next day in the early morning before the sun rose, I took a bus ride back home. On the way home, I felt rushed, very annoyed because the bus seemed to move so slowly, and there were so many stops along the way, making the journey feel never ending.

When I arrived home, I had some knowledge of English learned from middle school, so I decided to read the letter. It was written in both Korean and English.

The letter: "The employee below will return to Korea before the contract expires."

After reading the letter, I thought:

"Is that it? Just one short line?"

I felt a little strange the letter was so short. But, anyhow, my mom, my sister three years older than I, my brother a year younger than me, and my younger sister five years younger than I, all of us were so excited when we found out our father would be returning shortly. We were talking about our father and wondered.

The Family: "What we are going to do? We all go to picnic together?" and "What kind of gifts will he bring to us?"

We celebrated that night with storytelling and happy cloud dance in the flower-field, leaping, and jumping for joy.

My mom is an elegant, beautiful Korean woman with fair skin, a petite stature, and a slender figure. She is kind, friendly, and an excellent conversationalist. Of her growing time just like the people of her generation used to say she was born as a "useless girl," in a family of male dominance, with an older brother above her and a younger brother below her. She grew up discriminated and victimized by Korean culture of that time because she was female.

YOU'RE THE USELESS SECOND DAUGHTER

I visited my grandmother's house during my middle school summer break, that is my mother's mother, where she lived with my oldest uncle. He raised cattle and worked on a farm. When my grandmother bought us a bag of candy or snacks, she gave each of us one piece, and gave the rest of bag to my uncle's son.

In that rural setting, there were three daughters of my uncle and aunt, who lived with my grandmother. When she addressed her granddaughters, she always started with an irritated expression and angry saying, "You useless girls!" and then she would raise her voice with strong words.

Even our kind-hearted mom, who learned and grew up with my grandmother's behavior, when she got that angry she would scream at the top of her lungs. Our friends who used to come over still talk about my mother's loud voice.

My friends: "We were really scared of your mom's shouting; it was no joke."

As I am an adult, no matter what topic someone is talking about, as soon as their voice starts to rise and they begin speaking loudly, whether it's relevant or not, we all lose control and intense feeling of anger rise from the pit of our stomachs.

Those of us who are sensitive to loud noises, especially who are owners of loud voices, try to avoid making friends with them as much as possible.

The Confucian ideology was related to the livelihood of the common people of that era, making it a very important philosophy for them. If they had daughters, they were raised to be married off to someone else so they could not support her in her old age. As per the grandmother's words, which meant they were considered very "useless" women. During that era, many commoners with lower education likely thought and lived in a similar way.

Furthermore, they believed that having a son was a way to secure stability in their old age and their financial future, so initially, they favored having sons. It wasn't pleasant to see gender discrimination at my young age. The grandson she raised had all our candies, not even taking care of her when he grew up as an adult.

I would like to briefly talk about the story my mother told me when I was a newborn. My parents got married and had their first child, a daughter. They were a little disappointed but happy with having a daughter as their first child because she was adorable. And they didn't mind at the time because there would be more chances to have sons in the future. Then, three years later, I was born, and I was also a daughter.

I was born late in the evening around eleven o'clock p.m., just a day before the busy Korean New Year's Day. They were supposed to perform the ancestral rites and prepare food offerings for ancestors to the good luck and prosperity for the coming year.

But because a baby was born, they couldn't do it and wasted all the prepared food and time. My father was deeply disappointed with me because I was a girl and didn't even look at me and let alone hold me. My mother was angry with my father and complained about it.

Mother: "Honey! Did I give birth to this child alone? What's wrong with the child? You don't even look at her or hold her!"

A few days later, I stopped breastfeeding, didn't drink mother's milk from mother, and I slept for three days. My parents were frightened; they decided to call a shaman, as there were no doctors in the rural area at the time. My father had to walk for miles, walk through the long rice field and cross a small mountain to reach a shaman.

The shaman who arrived at the house examined me and prayed whether the baby would be alive or dead before performing the rituals and treatments. Then, he performed the acupuncture for urgent cases only: the shaman began placing needles to vital points of my body, on my throat, starting from the center of my face. After a while, I woke up from sleep. I started to cry, and the crying sounded like a duck's quacking.

The shaman, looking angry, turned to my father, and asked:

"Did you do something disrespectful on your way to bring me here?"

My father replied: "Actually, as I was passing through the rice field, there was a duck quacking after being hit by a gun, and I felt bad wasting good duck's meat, so I stopped by my friend's house to have a drink with it later. Then, I came to pick you up, Mr. Shaman."

Mother knew that my throat was dry after not eating for three days. She carefully moistened my lips with a spoonful of her milk. It wasn't long before I finally snapped up her breast to start to breastfeeding from mother again.

WISE MOTHER

My mother said she never had the chance to attend the school she desperately wanted. She wanted to go to school so badly that she even scratched her father's legs until they bled while begging to be sent to school, but she was not allowed to go.

She had to self-educate herself, and to put it in the context of a kindergarten student who couldn't even write properly. She could barely write with a few strokes and words, but she was able to read and write in Korean. She was a typical homemaker, taking care of the house and raising the children.

My mother lived with me in the United States for several years. During that time, there was a moment when she asked me to teach her some basic conversational English. She learned a few basic sentences for minimal communication and her pronunciation was exceptional, almost on par with a native speaker.

She also managed to pass her driver's license exam on the first try. She practiced whenever she had spare time, self-taught herself the English alphabets, and even attended an ESL (English as a second language) school to improve her basic conversational skills. My mother was a very wise and smart lady. I remember discussing a concern with her when I was in the sixth grade of elementary school.

Me: "Mom, why do I have a flat nose? I'm so worried!"

Most mothers might have responded out of annoyance, saying something like this.

Typical mom: "You were born that way, so what can you do? You can get plastic surgery when you earn money later!"

But my mother responded differently.

Mom: "When you were born, your eyes, nose and mouth were very distinct, and you were so beautiful but now, as you keep growing. When you go to the bathroom, while you are sitting there to poop, hold a toothpick with your teeth and pull your nose forward until you are done pooping. This way, it might grow bigger."

Since then, I sat in a corner of the yard where the outhouse was, looking at the ground below to see feces, and every time I strained, I pulled on my nose about ten times. In the hot summer months of July and August, I sweated and smelled of poop while stretching my nose. I did that for a several months, but my nose didn't get any bigger.

Not long after coming to the United States, I got my first eye exam and went to the optometrist to get glasses fitted. During the eye exam, the native English-speaking optometrist wanted to ask me something. I thought he had some questions to help me get better services, so I allowed it.

Optometrist: "May I touch your nose?"

The question piqued my complex and made me a little upset, and I thought to myself.

My thoughts: "Wow, even in the United States, someone is reminding me that my nose is flat!"

Now, I've been living in the United States for over thirty-five years, and Americans often say I am beautiful because I have a flat nose.

Talking about the outhouse brought back this memory.

As I became an adult, I used to bring about ten bananas as gifts for my mom whenever I went to see her at home. Bananas were expensive and hard to find during that time in Korea. My mom liked bananas, but she would hide them in the deep recesses of the attic and never ate them. She didn't give them to us either.

You had to open a small door near the bedroom and climb several stairs to reach the tiny attic, which was my mom's treasure trove. The bananas that were hidden there were given as occasional gifts to only two special people.

The outhouse cleaner and the garbage collectors.

Me: "Why give those expensive bananas to the outhouse cleaners and the garbage collectors?!"

My mom responded:

"They are poor, and they work so hard."

My mom always felt compassion for those who were less fortunate or worked horrendously. She may have recently heard about the Deuteronomy sermon at the church in the past weeks.

I'm reminded of a particular Bible verse.

> [7] If anyone is poor among your fellow Israelites in any of the towns of the land the Lord your God is giving you, do not be hardhearted or tightfisted toward them. [8] Rather, be openhanded and freely lend them whatever they need.
>
> [9] Be careful not to harbor this wicked thought: "The seventh year, the year for canceling debts, is near," so that you do not show ill will toward the needy among your fellow Israelites and give them nothing. They may then appeal to the Lord against you, and you will be found guilty of sin.
>
> [10] Give generously to them and do so without a grudging heart; then because of this the Lord your God will bless you in all your work and in everything you put your hand to. [11] There will always be poor people on the land. Therefore, I command you to be openhanded toward your fellow Israelites who are poor and needy in your land. (Deut 15:7–11)

Sometimes, when I go to the stores or gas stations, I encounter young people in between their twenties or thirties, who are usually begging. I used to see them and think like this.

Past me: "They are young, and they should find a job and work instead of begging here!! I don't want to waste my money!"

Then I would either pretend not to see them or just walk by, thinking they were pathetic. However, at some point, they began to appear to me as Jesus. It appears he was standing in front of me with filthy clothing on the beggar's body to give me an opportunity to bless me. Every time this happens, I give the money for a meal, and it feels like I can hear the money sound going into my heaven bank.

CHARMING FATHER

Now it's time for my father's story. My father was average height and quite handsome. He had a strong charismatic voice, and he was born with a natural sense of humor that made his storytelling very entertaining. It was not uncommon for our parents' friends and couples to visit our house almost daily.

On those occasions, my siblings and I would be chased out to other rooms. We couldn't understand why they always came to our house and left their own homes behind. Everyone seemed to enjoy their gatherings, singing, playing cards, and there was always hearty laughter filling the air.

Moreover, I didn't understand the reasons why those wives would visit our house to meet my mother even on weekdays when the husbands were at work all the time like they lived in our house. During the summertime, our family, along with those six families of our parents, would pack up a variety of foods and head to a nearby valley for a picnic.

We would cook the same menu every year, chicken porridge with added red pepper paste. Since the water in the valley was not deep enough for swimming, we couldn't swim. However, everyone would put their swimsuits on and have fun jumping from rock to rock in the shallow flowing water. It was quite enjoyable; we all had fun and were happy.

My father was knowledgeable and studied various texts and books such as the Analects of Confucius, Mencius, the great learning, and the Doctrine of the Mean. He also delved into astrology and studied physiognomy, and many people sought his advice for naming their children.

My father enjoyed taking photographs, and there are several pictures in a old album of him and mother taking photos together at the memorable services held at places. My father was a very affectionate person.

When my siblings were growing up, Korea was very poor. We didn't have toys or pretty dolls to play with. Our doll play involved cutting out paper doll illustrations and dressing them in paper clothes. I used to watch my friends play with those cut off paper dolls. I remember they were too expensive for us to buy them.

There weren't many delicious snacks, candies, or munchies then either. I remember a few snacks, candies like big-eyed candies with coarse sugar, mom-mom biscuits crackers, golden man bubble gum, and other treats that we could buy for around fifty won, equivalent to three cents in a dollar. Additionally, on the street corner, there was a vendor who melted sugar over a coal fire and mixed it with baking soda to make a candy called "Dalgona," which means "sweet."

When our father was going to work in the morning, my sisters, brother, and I used to line up on the edge of the house's wooden veranda, extending our right arms and reaching out our hands toward him.

Father would turn around and give each of us a one hundred won coin; it was about ten cents in a dollar. On his way back from work, he always brought fruits, rice cakes, and other snacks for us.

I don't remember this, but according to my older sister, when she had a school picnic, father would buy her bag of snacks to carry along. Whenever the opportunity arose, he would give us hugs and kisses. He loved us all very much without any discrimination.

At that time growing up, some of my school friends graduated from high school, but due to family circumstances, not every one of my friends could attend college. My siblings and I wanted to go to college, and if we were accepted, our parents would support our education. Our parents never forced us to become something they wanted us to be. They allowed us to pursue our own paths and passion in life.

They simply provided us with financial support according to our interest and strengths, allowing us to pursue what we found interesting, excelled at, wanted to do. Our father always urged our mother to do so.

Once, my mother said:

"Your father has studied a lot and has a lot of knowledge, therefore his problem-solving might take a while, but since I didn't go to school and have an empty head that has a lot of room, I can quickly resolve things well."

LONGING

While my father was overseas, it wasn't possible to make international phone calls then. Sometimes he would record his voice messages and send them along with packages. Everyone in the family listened to these voice messages on a Walkman cassette player, repeatedly. There was even a time when the cassette player broke down due to over-usage.

He also sent some pictures taken with native people wearing traditional clothing of that country; it feels strange to see them dressed in what looked like bed sheets over them, on their head white turbans, and Arabian attire with sunglasses.

Our family gathered in Mom's bedroom to write a response to my father's letter. We laid on the warm bedroom floor and each of us wrote a letter to him.

While my mom wanted to write many letters, she struggled with expressing herself in Korean. She hesitated several times and eventually asked one of us to write the letter on her behalf.

My father always sent us two letters, one to my mom and the other one to us. In one to Mother, he told Mom not to worry if she couldn't write in Korean perfectly and asked her to write a letter the best she could. Throughout that period, our family accumulated a lot of letters filled with our memories and painted those on the life canvas for longing.

THE LETTER

    Before my father's overseas assignment, we didn't have an electric rice cooker. During those times, my mother would prepare the rice even on days when my father couldn't come home and put it deep inside the closet under the blankets, making sure it stayed warm just in case Father came home unannounced. My mother and father seemed to love each other very much.

    I can't help and wonder how much my father missed my mother and us while working abroad. And my mom, how many unspoken words did my mother have and want to share with my father in the letters, raising four young children alone? How much did she miss him when she prepared the foods he loved? When I think about these things, tears come to my eyes.

CHAPTER 2

Lightning Strike

FATHER'S RETURN TO KOREA

Upon hearing the news that my father would be returning early, I rejoiced and returned to my aunt's house to prepare for my entry into high school. According to my sister, after receiving a delivered letter stating that my father would be coming back to Korea early, my mother and sister were planning to go to the airport to welcome him. Instead, a few days later my mother received a call from his company instructing her to come in the company headquarters.

After receiving the call, my mother headed to the headquarters in Seoul. Meanwhile, my sister, who had been busy preparing for her senior year of high school, received a message from her school principal to go to my father's company immediately. When my sister arrived at the headquarters, the company employees escorted her to a nearby hotel.

Upon arriving at the hotel, went up to one of the guest rooms, and opening the door to a room, she found my mother unconscious and lying on the bed. The joy and excitement of finally reuniting with her husband, whom she had longed for in her dreams, was shattered when she received the lighting strike news of my father's death at the company headquarters. The shock was so overwhelming that she fainted right there, and the company staff had to transfer her to the nearby hotel. Mom would have had such poignant and heart-wrenching thoughts rushing through her mind as she collapsed.

"Now, I can neither see nor meet my dearly missed husband, the warm and affectionate father whom the children love, the generous and kind-hearted man to big brother, the big brother who loved his sister since she was young. The witty and eloquent man who was popular with friends, the handsome and intelligent man with a charming voice, the young man at thirty-nine years of age that longed to see by everyone . . . ."

After hearing the news of my father's death, I attended the high school entrance ceremony alone where no one from my family came. For a few months, I felt like I was living as an empty and soulless person, just walking around with my body. My mind was blank, and I couldn't focus my eyes on anything. It seemed like there was nothing visible through my eyes.

FORTY PILLS A DAY

After a few months had passed by I returned home going to school from there. When I came back from school, my mother wouldn't eat and continued drinking several bottles of soju (soju is distilled, like vodka) every day. In the morning, she would wake up hung over, which caused the headaches and dizziness due to alcohol consumption. She started to take pain relievers, enormous amount pills, over forty pills a day.

She purchased so much of the pain medication from the pharmacy they even sold pills to her at discounted prices. Mom gave up her daily life and her duty as a mother to us. We had to prepare our own meals, do laundry, and pack our own lunchboxes for school. A month later, my father's belongings arrived.

My father asked us to make a wish list of things we wanted and include them in the letters. I remember that I wished for a watch. The package arrived in an incredibly tiny box, containing only a minuscule amount.

I think my father, who had a good personality and was fun to be with, would have had many friends from work. He would have spent his free time on weekends shopping for his beloved family and showed all the gifts to his friends, and those would bring big smiles to his face as he told them about the gifts.

Father: "How about this one, for my second daughter? The watch with an illustration of an Arabian scene on the golden background. She will probably like it when I give it to her in Korea. Hahaha."

During that time, I'm sure he would have been very happy buying gifts for each family member one by one. He often explained in his letters when he had purchased special items for us.

My gift, the beautiful watch with an Arabian scene on the golden background, was in part of his belongings. But only a few gifts and there were no expensive items like the high-value decorations and cameras that father had mentioned. The family was puzzled seeing very a small amount of Father's belongings. Our family was very disappointed missing some of his items.

While Father's belongings were being sorted by his company in that country, going through customs and the main office, someone stole some of his items. It's hard to imagine that someone would commit such an act knowing that those were the belongings of a deceased person and it would cause grief to his family. We were too young to understand it fully, but I can't help but wonder how much of sense of betrayal Mother must have felt once again.

Your husband was taken away, and the remaining belongings were stolen once again. Mother would be incredibly unjust and frustrated. Those individuals who were responsible for that will carry the memory of their actions and God knows too. I am reminded of several Bible verses related to orphans and widows.

> And the Levite, because he has no portion or inheritance with you, and the sojourner, the fatherless, and the widow, who are within your towns, shall come and eat and

> be filled, that the Lord your God may bless you in all the work of your hands that you do. (Deut 14:29)
>
> When you reap your harvest in your field and forget a sheaf in the field, you shall not go back to get it. It shall be for the sojourner, the fatherless, and the widow, that the Lord your God may bless you in all the work of your hands. (Deut 24:19)
>
> Cursed be anyone who perverts the justice due to the sojourner, the fatherless, and the widow. And all the people shall say, "Amen." (Deut 27:19)

Our God, compassionate and helpful, who comforts and assists the weak and the helpless, our God, my God! I pray for them.

God, our Father, for reasons unknown to us, forgive those who, in a moment of poor judgment, laid hands on the possessions of others. Lead them to repent and guide them towards the right path so they can help others struggling, less fortunate neighbors with goods several times what was taken, in the name of Jesus. Amen.

Afterward, my mom sometimes said, "My insides have all rotted away!" And my dad used to say to us since we were young, "I will die at thirty-nine." At that time, when I was in elementary school, I couldn't understand why my dad would say such a thing. I didn't even ask why.

FINAL FAREWELL

After some time, my father's body arrived, and the whole family and close relatives gathered in a hospital viewing room. While the preparations were underway, the children were waiting outside. At that moment, my younger sister, who was ten years old, asked a question.

My sister: "Sis, is this dad's coffin?"

The coffin placed at one end of the hospital wall had my father's name written in English. I replied as follows.

Me: "No, it's not. It doesn't look like Dad's; it's someone else's."

I didn't want my younger sister to acknowledge that it was our father's coffin, perhaps because it was too painful. After a while, someone gestured for us to come inside. We entered the viewing room.

A hospital staff member removed the white sheet that had covered our father. We saw our father's lifeless body lying on the low hospital bed, wearing only underwear, as if he were peacefully asleep.

There were bruises all over his body, some as large as apples, especially on his chest and abdomen. It was explained that the rock truck had overturned, and the weight of stones had crushed him. I was just fifteen years old, a freshman in high school, and I couldn't help but think:

"Is this the last time I'll see my beloved father? Are his face, voice, and loving hugs all disappearing now? From this moment on, we won't be able to see his affectionate gaze either. I don't want to say goodbye. Dad, please stay with us."

I had a lump in my throat, and I sobbed as I held onto my uncle, who was standing beside me.

Since then, I've been susceptible to stress due to post-traumatic stress disorder (PTSD). As I go through life, events similar to my father's death or even smaller incidents can trigger intense stress reactions, making them feel like real situations, and I respond with heightened sensitivity.

In other words, due to the lingering psychological shock from that time, various symptoms of PTSD manifest within me. Unwanted thoughts keep intruding into my mind, making it difficult for me to get a peaceful night's sleep. These events replay as if they were happening right next to me, and it feels like an incessant, repetitive cycle.

When these symptoms occur, life becomes challenging for several days or even weeks. During the day, I try to keep busy at work or at home, which helps to keep my thoughts distracted and things seem somewhat normal. However, as the night falls and I lay down in a quiet bed, the symptoms intensify, and it becomes agonizing.

As a result, I struggle to get a good night's sleep, and in search of a solution, I read several self-help books recommended by mental health professionals. Among the books I read, I found a method that has been helpful for me. The technique involves creating a different scenario in me to halt the constant replay of distressing thoughts when I lay in bed at night.

In other words, to stop the distressing thoughts in bed, I need to retrace my thoughts in reverse from where I started thinking about them. Doing so helps to genuinely disperse those thoughts. However, if my thoughts persist, I get out of bed and go to the kitchen or another room and engage in a different activity to help stop the thoughts.

A few years ago, I consulted my primary care physician due to these symptoms, which caused me distress and anxiety. The doctor diagnosed me with mental distress and prescribed medication. My family has healed from the emotional wounds of my father's death and is leading a normal life. However, these scars still linger in our hearts, and any significant or minor stress can trigger PTSD symptoms. These scars have become a part of my life, just like the physical ones on my skin.

PTSD SCARS

A significant event that triggered my PTSD scars happened in South Korea.

"On Saturday, October 29, 2022, in Itaewon, Yongsan-gu, Seoul, South Korea, a stampede incident occurred during a Halloween festival in the narrow alley west of Hamilton Hotel in Itaewon's global food alley. It became the worst and largest-scale stampede incident in South Korean history, resulting in the tragic death of 159 individuals."

Although the incident had no direct connection to me or my family, upon learning about it, I felt as though the air was being squeezed out of me. It was as if something had struck my chest with force.

The thoughts of this event and the images associated with it stayed in my mind at work and at home for a whole week. The pictures I saw in the news made me feel as though I had been present in that situation, and this troubled me for some time.

As I wrote the above text, I considered that God has blessed us with gift of memory, which is a wonderful aspect of our human nature. It helps us in our studies and everyday life. However, it's also a reminder that as time goes on, our memories fade, and there are things we can't remember.

Especially those memories we'd rather not dwell on tend to become less vivid and less significant as time passes. It's a way in which we gradually forget, allowing us to move forward and not be burdened by the past. I am grateful to God for this aspect of our human experience.

My father was buried in the ancestral burial ground of the Lee family in Mount Seon. I continued my life as a first-year high school student. I wrote a few pages of an essay titled "The Lonely Oak Tree" and gave it to the teacher. A few days later, my worried homeroom teacher visited our house. At that time, I was silently experiencing inexplicable tears, a sense of desolation, depression, and suffering from PTSD symptoms.

As days and months passed, one day, I was walking towards the bus stop for an after-school bus. About one hundred meters ahead, my father was walking towards me. Inside, I said to myself, "Father, you're dead, aren't you? How are you approaching me?" I felt a mixture of joyous excitement and sorrow, as if a whirlwind of emotions was sweeping through me.

As the approaching figure resembling my father got closer, I couldn't contain my joy and happiness, and a broad smile filled my face. As he got nearer, at around five meters, three meters, and about one meter away, the person turned out to be a stranger whom I had never seen before. Perhaps it was as if God had sent my father's angel to me, conveying a final message through such heartfelt emotions.

Father's Angel: "My beloved daughter, it's time to let me go now. I know how much you loved me; how much you missed me.

I saw your tears and grieved with you. I witnessed your pain. From now on, you need to live your life to the fullest. I love you, my daughter."

After that moment, I slowly began to recover from my PTSD symptoms.

Afterwards, I worked diligently on studying and practicing typing and I became proficient at it. I even begged my mom to purchase an English typewriter, equivalent to a month's salary for an average company employee, and practiced typing tirelessly.

I even helped a church pastor with a substantial amount of his English graduation thesis. Over the years, typing has been a skill I value, and it has been significantly helpful during my time working at US companies. I'll briefly introduce post-traumatic stress disorder (PTSD).

This condition includes recurrent, distressing memories of past events that feel like real situations, severe anxiety, and uncontrollable thoughts related to traumatic events when under stress. Most people temporarily lose their ability to cope due to shocking events, but it can improve over time with proper management. Furthermore, if we investigate it more specifically, there could be seventeen different symptoms associated with it.

1. Agitation
2. Nervousness and anxiety
3. Thinking or concentration problems
4. Memory problems
5. Headaches
6. Depression
7. Suicidal thoughts
8. Mood swings
9. Obsessive compulsive tendencies
10. Panic
11. Paranoia

12. Shakiness
13. Substance abuse
14. Flashbacks
15. Hypervigilance
16. Nightmares
17. Sleep disturbances

CHAPTER 3

My Second Parents

COVETOUS INDIVIDUALS

I didn't want to go home after school because life there was difficult. My mom had given up on life, she didn't cook, and the smell of her alcohol consumption was unpleasant. Our daily routine involved her being drunk, vomiting, and lying down, and it was challenging. Moreover, her drinking made her irritable.

And she would often hit us for trivial reasons. She hit us frequently, leaving bruises on my thighs, and when she didn't have the strength to continue hitting, she would pinch us forcefully with her fingers until our skin turned purple.

The next day, our body would be covered in bruises from her pinches and sometimes from her pulling hair, but strangely, she didn't slap us. We didn't resist or say anything when she hit us, we simply took the beatings. We couldn't understand our mom's actions, but we knew the real underlying cause behind it all.

My mom would get so angry that she continued to hit us, and at times, she'd even froth at the mouth and collapse when she lost control. The abuse from my mom persisted. My ten-year-old younger sister was so terrified of those times that she wanted to hide anywhere away from mom and live without speaking to avoid getting hit by our mom.

One of the sayings in the Talmud goes, "When the devil is busy finding people, he sends alcohol to people." I was amazed at how our small and frail mom could derive such strength from somewhere and it us so forcefully when she was drunk. I'm not here to expose my mother's child abuse to the world. Instead, I want to share the story of how our family has lived with mental illnesses after the shock of my father's death during my childhood.

I still really miss my mom. I will meet again and love my poor and pitiable mom in heaven, and I loved her then and still do now.

At that time, there was no one among our relatives or the adults around us with the knowledge to advise and help my mom that she should seek a doctor's help. When my father was dead, his friends and their wives, who used to visit our home frequently, never came to visit or console my mother.

According to my sister, my father's life insurance paid a small amount, enough to consider starting a small boarding school. There were discussions about using that money for such a purpose. However, my mom, who had not received a basic education, had no formal qualifications or work experience, and was likely to be frightened about what kind of business venture to start.

Later, my greedy uncle gathered relatives for a meeting to "help" us. As a result of this meeting, they decided that the only house we had was transferred to my mom's as well as the names of us four children, because they feared my mom might sell the house, leave us behind, and disappear. After my mom's passing, it became quite complicated and required time and money to change the ownership records that had been set up.

During this time, my uncle, however, wanted my mom to give him a certain portion of the insurance money. Meanwhile, various relatives and neighbors, drawn by the scent of money, kept coming to ask for financial assistance, like flies swarming around sweet food. Among them a distant relative opened not one but two pastry shops with the money and earned a significant profit.

Initially, they would give me a bag of bread as a gift when I went to collect the interest and they did provide the interest fairly for a while. However, it didn't take long for them to start complaining, saying that had paid more in interest than the principal, and they stopped repaying the borrowed money altogether. Nevertheless, we managed to get by for several years through this interesting game, putting all the children through college with the earnings.

Mom continued to drink, and we, feeling like orphans with or without her, often brought homemade food to school, consisting of simple dishes like kimchi and potatoes with onions. In the evenings, we'd make dumplings or noodles with potatoes and onions, which the four siblings shared.

Sometimes, we'd fry up onions, sprinkle them with red pepper paste, and eat them as a side dish with kimchi fried rice. When we were hungry, we'd slice up raw radishes or sweet potatoes to eat in the evening. My older sister, who was in her final year of high school, took on the responsibility of cooking for us and doing the laundry. She had a strong sense of responsibility, and Mom often relied on her for help.

Due to my mom's alcohol addiction and her neglect of her children, my uncle's family, who is my mom's younger brother, moved to the adjacent room. My aunt ran a snack shop in front of school. They moved in with us and took care of our meals and laundry. They played the role of our second parents for several years.

Even as we grew up and became adults, my siblings who still live in Korea always consider our aunt and uncle as our parents during holidays and birthdays. My siblings in Korea never miss visiting their home. Whenever I think about them, I call my aunt and uncle in Korea to express my gratitude for raising us.

ADOPTED DAUGHTER

When I was four years old, I almost went to my greedy uncle's house to live as their adopted daughter. They were very eager to have a child, especially a son, and it wasn't because my family was struggling financially.

However, since my younger sibling was a son and they couldn't give him away, my parents and my uncle agreed that I would be sent to live with them for two years as a sort of foster child. While living there, I made friends, and I have fond memories of the house owner's daughter, who would take me to various places because she liked me.

At that time, my older sister, who was attending elementary school, told me that she was worried about me, missed me, and wanted to see her younger sister, who she was afraid might be taken away. So, she took the train all by herself to find the place where my uncle lived far away. She remembered coming to visit me, playing together for a while, and then returning home.

My uncle's wife gave me a perky and cute bobbed haircut, dressed me in several lovely dresses, bought me a small child-sized handbag that looked like a mini market basket with little holes in plastic, and even got me shiny pretty shoes. She always made sure I looked well dressed, and I remember her carrying me around like a trophy as we traveled to various places riding trains together.

One day, when I returned to my uncle's house after playing outside with my friends, I found that the tall iron gate was firmly locked. I knocked on the gate several times, but it remained closed. I waited for a long time outside the gate. After a while, I heard my uncle's wife's voice from inside, speaking in a soft whisper.

Uncle's wife: "If you call me 'Mom,' I'll open the door for you. Come on, try calling me 'Mom.'"

At that moment, I realized that she wasn't my real mother but rather my uncle's wife. I found it strange that she insisted on me calling her mom. I couldn't bring myself to call her that; I remained silent and waited at the door until she decided to open the door.

On that day, I was so upset that I banged my head against the wall of my uncle's room and ended up inhaling coal gas while sleeping. That led to carbon monoxide poisoning. My uncle used a charcoal heating system to heat the room. And I was rushed to the emergency room. When I regained consciousness, I found myself coming back to uncle's house and being carried on my uncle's back. From that day on, I cried and threw a fit, demanding to be brought back home; finally, I returned home.

A few years later, my uncle adopted a boy born to a woman who worked at a bar. That boy was strong and had a small stature from a young age. He was very skilled in calculations. Every time I visit my uncle's house, I could feel that that boy was quite different from other kids. As he grew older, I heard that he got involved in gambling at casinos and even escaped to Macau. And then, a few years later, my uncle finally had a daughter.

WHAT IS YOUR TRUE NAME?

I am a Korean, and was born as a second daughter into a family where I was not welcomed and as a female, through no choices I made. Being born as a female is not a sin.

I was born as a second daughter, and I couldn't change that. However, in those days when my father desired a son, he gave me an additional nickname that indicated the hope of having a son in the future. As a result, my parents went on to have younger brothers born under my second nickname a year later.

My second name, the nickname, is the name that family and relatives called me right after I was born. It will be used until the end of my life. My registered name was considered pretty by my friends, but it became a source of teasing from my elementary school classmates, who found it like a cosmetics brand name. So, I once consulted my mom for a solution.

Jennifer: "Mom, kids make fun of me because my name sounds like a makeup brand!"

Mom: "If they tease you, tell them to stop. And if they continue, give them a little pinch!"

Once when I was in middle school, my aunt was visiting our house. I received a call from a friend of mine at school, and when my aunt answered the phone, she said, 'There's a girl on the line asking for so and so. Who could that be?

Even our aunt didn't know my real name. When I came to the United States and applied for US citizenship, there was a question asking, if I wanted to change my name. I didn't hesitate at all. I considered it an opportunity for a fresh start in life, and I was genuinely happy to be able to change my name.

I marked "Yes" on the citizenship application form and borrowed a book of names from the library to choose a name. I selected a name for myself from the book with the number one ranking for girls' names from 1970 to 1984, which is the name I use now.

I chose that name because I liked one of its meanings. The name's meaning is described as follows, and I changed my name to Jennifer: "(blessed spirit) One selected and favored by God, and bearing a mission and meaning to perform, a blessed soul." When people at work or in church ask about my Korean name, I don't tell it to them. The meaningless name that isn't called by family is not real to me. My real name is Jennifer, a blessed soul.

POOR BEAR

Once, when I was in the third year of middle school, I visited my uncle's, his house in the back, and I saw a four-year-old boy living there with uncle's mother-in-law. After hearing the story, I found out that, the son, whom I used to call "uncle," while he lived in mother-in-law's house had a child outside of wedlock.

The mother-in-law brought the child along to live with them. However, due to conflicts between mother-in-law and daughter-in-law, regarding favor to the four-year-old boy, discrimination to her granddaughters, and disagreements with the mother-in-law, they were eventually driven out of the house and had to live with my uncle.

After being driven out of the house, the mother-in-law vented her anger on that child, abusing him by burning his hand and arm with cigarettes. The nameless and unrecognized child was called Gom (Bear). Even after many years have passed, this remains a heartbreaking and painful memory etched in my mind.

The question arises whether the desire for a child, the uncle's wife, leading to this situation, could have been influenced by her own mother. If they believed in Jesus, would they have made such choices? The Bible, which contains God's word, clearly describes what greed and desires are and how to deal with them, doesn't it?

In my opinion, people often tend to narrowly interpret the word "greed" in financial terms. My definition of greed goes beyond just monetary matters. It involves the excessive desire and attachment to cross the boundaries with anything. Whether it's for basic necessities and the continuous pursuit of wanting to possess and enjoy.

Galatians 5:16–24 from the Bible, as translated in the New International Version (NIV), reads:

> So, I say, walk by the Spirit, and you will not gratify the desires of the flesh. For the flesh desires what is contrary to the Spirit, and the Spirit what is contrary to the flesh. They conflict with each other so that you are not to do whatever you want. But if you are led by the Spirit, you are not under the law.
>
> The acts of the flesh are obvious: sexual immorality, impurity, and debauchery; idolatry and witchcraft; hatred, discord, jealousy, fits of rage, selfish ambition, dissensions, factions, and envy; drunkenness, orgies, and the like. I warn you, as I did before, that those who live like this will not inherit the kingdom of God.
>
> But the fruit of the Spirit is love, joy, peace, forbearance, kindness, goodness, faithfulness, gentleness, and self-control. Against such things there is no law. Those who belong to Christ Jesus have crucified the flesh with its passions and desires.

These verses emphasize the contrast between living according to the desires of the flesh and living by the guidance of the Holy Spirit. The works of the flesh are contrasted with the fruit of the Spirit, which includes self-control among its attributes. Paul, the apostle, is admonishing the Galatians to choose the path of the Spirit over the desires of the flesh.

In other words, I also want to say that it's about the selfish desires for possession or achievement, excluding natural instincts.

In a previous article I read, it discussed the reasons for child abuse and behaviors classified as child abuse.

Child abuse is unquestionably a wrong committed by adults who are parents and have become mature individuals. Absolutely, the cause of child abuse is not within the child; claiming that the child's actions provided the starting point is simply an excuse and a rationalization.

Child abuse perpetrators are often individuals with poor emotional regulation skills. Essentially, they cannot control their impulses or anger and resort to cruel methods, abusing children. According to one study, those who engage in child abuse also have a higher rate of depression.

Furthermore, these parents may experience anxiety about whether their child's behavior will ever improve, which can also be a stress factor. Being impulsive and lacking self-control, they don't attempt to correctly address the problems at hand but instead aim for quick closure.

In this case, parents report using violence that should never be employed with their children, instilling fear in them to halt their actions. Here, parents may mistakenly believe that the children have learned their lesson, using discipline as an excuse. However, children only stop due to fear, without understanding what they did wrong or the context of the situation.

Therefore, true discipline can be considered imparting to the child the things they should avoid doing and the things they should abide by, rather than relying on emotions.

Furthermore, perpetrators often tend to pursue an idealized image of children. When the child does not behave as they wish, they can experience severe anxiety. This can lead to low self-esteem and high feelings of inferiority. Committing abuse may also be a way for them to assert control over what they see as weaker individuals, particularly children, to boost their lost self-esteem.

They may claim they are disciplining the child for the child's own growth, but in most cases, it is often just a way for them to release their stress. Even if a small percentage of cases were genuinely for stress relief, it still constitutes child abuse. Punishment or violence directed at children, regardless of the stated intent, is considered child abuse.

DISCIPLINE OF AMERICAN PEOPLE

Once, an American friend visited our house with her four-year-old son. My friend and I were engaged in discussions about shopping and various topics of today's world. Bored, her son found our Korean furniture and items quite fascinating.

And he began touching things placed on top of them. My friend warned him not to touch them, but at his curious age, he paid a little attention to her words and continued exploring our living room. Finally, my friend, losing her patience, called her son over and told him this.

Friend: "Sit here for five minutes without moving!!"
Son: "No! I don't want to sit, Mom."
Friend: "This is a consequence for not listening to me!"
Son: "Please—Mom . . . I don't want to sit—"

At this point, the son started crying, but the friend sternly taught him the lesson, saying that if he didn't sit quietly, the time would be extended. In less than a minute, the son struggled to get up. He couldn't move, so he shook his legs on both sides to release his energy.

I've read newspaper articles where a young daughter was made to stand for hours, causing significant physical problems. While I believe that discipline and educating children with a few minutes of punishment without physically harming them are acceptable methods of raising children, if parents find it difficult to control their emotions and anger towards their children's actions, they should reconsider their using this disciplinary approach.

As children grow older, they play, jump around, roll on beds, and dance, using their abundant energy to keep their heart healthy, promote cell division, develop muscles, and gradually progress in physical development. Continuously expelling the remaining energy to generate even greater energy, they should grow according to the natural order created by God.

Another form of discipline is the United States is making a child stand still, facing the wall, and parents forcing them to reflect until they have repented. This punishment is one that truly requires patience from children and is one of the most detested forms of discipline. It is typically used by parents for younger children before they become teenagers; it is usually despised by children.

CHAPTER 4

Family Evangelism

MOTHER AND FATHER

This is a story from a few years ago before my father passed away. My father didn't really enforce things; he was always proud of my older sister, who was diligent, did well in her studies, and was gentle. On one evening during her first year of high school, my sister came back home after going to church.

My father got very angry with her and scolded her, with lightning words. He said. "You're the age to study, so why are you going to church? What's this? Stop going there right now, do you hear me?"

He was always a loving father, giving each of us one hundred won for our daily allowance every morning before going to work. During the Olympics, he once brought a beautiful white sweater with colorful Olympic patterns embroidered on it as a gift for us three daughters.

I had never seen our kind father raise his voice or shout at my older sister. Seeing him like that was both startling and terrifying. As a result, my other siblings and I were too scared to go to church.

During that time, my older sister began to receive my father's persecution because of her involvement with Jesus. She was always caught when she went to church, and my father's outbursts continued. However, my sister persisted and kept attending church. She deeply desired to attend a retreat held at the church, but my father's opposition prevented her from participating, leaving her feeling quite frustrated.

I don't have personal memories of this, but according to what my older sister told me, she used to take us to church when she was in elementary school. She had a rough appearance, uncombed hair, and sometimes didn't clean herself like most kids in that era about the same.

She'd hold the hands of us, her younger siblings, who were around three years of age at the time. We'd go to church together. She mentioned that it was enjoyable to receive pencils and school supplies there. After church, she would often take us to a nearby park to play together. After father's passing my younger brother, youngest sister, and I started attending church due to my sister's evangelizing.

However, after our father's death, my mother was engulfed in grief, and her daily drinking, along with the fear of her physical punishment to us, made the idea of going to church impossible. Our uncle and his family moved in, and prepared our meals, so the issue of food was resolved. But my mother's alcohol abuse persisted.

And three years passed. One day something significant happened: a pastor came to our house to visit my mother. He entered the room where the strong smell of alcohol lingered and began the conversation.

Pastor: "You've been through a lot of sadness, haven't you?"

He said, as he talked about my younger sister, who was in the fifth grade at the time, "Your youngest daughter comes to morning prayers every day and cries, praying for you. She's been so scared of you drinking for years and hitting her sisters. 'Please, Jesus, save our mother . . . ,' she said, 'please, don't let her hurt our sisters. God, please save her,' with tears streaming down her face."

After the pastor's visit, my mom was converted and embraced Jesus, and healing of God began. She quit drinking, stopped performing ancestral rituals, and earnestly started get to know Jesus and God. Whenever she felt anger toward us, she would endure it and pray. Hallelujah!!

I received Jesus into my life three years prior to my mother, attended church diligently, joined the choir, and enrolled to praise the Lord every Sunday. I didn't miss Bible study and read through the entire Bible several times.

Starting from a small tent church, our church has grown into a large congregation where many believers receive God's grace and go forth. Even today, when I visit Korea, I worship God in that church.

GIFTS OF THE HOLY SPIRIT

One autumn day, a revival was held at the church, and for a week, I listened to Pastor's sermons every day. One the last day of the revival, I felt the grace of the Holy Spirit covering the church like fire. It was as if the room of the last supper, Mark's upper room, the site of the gift of tongues, was manifested all around me.

And people were speaking in tongues from every direction. I fervently prayed to God, asking him to grant me the gift of speaking in tongues, but I was disappointed when it didn't happen, and I returned home with a heavy heart.

When I returned home, my fervent desire to receive the gift of speaking in tongues didn't fade away. I went to an empty room and began to pray with all my heart, pouring out my soul in sweat. As I continued to pray for some time, my eyes were closed but suddenly I felt a brilliant, indescribable white light surrounding me.

And then, like a bowling ball with tremendous force, a white fireball moving rapidly like a shooting star entered my mouth. Finally, I began speaking in tongues. I uttered incomprehensible sounds, beating like a drum, and the feeling came with a joy beyond any words can describes and a happiness in my soul as it praised the Lord. Afterward, I was so ecstatic, it felt like I was walking on a cloud, and every day was a day of joy.

From then on, my faith deepened day by day. I actively participated in church meetings, student gatherings, and even mountain prayer sessions led by the pastor, where I fervently prayed to God in both tongues and words. One day, during a mountain prayer session, a real language (a dialect) emerged, not just the "lalala" movement of the first speaking in tongues.

I didn't know which language I was speaking in tongues, but I recognized the phrase *xiexie*, which means "thank you" in Chinese, even though I hadn't learned Chinese before. I realized that many expressions of gratitude appeared within the tongues, which led me to understand that it was a Chinese dialect.

And then I graduated from high school and went on to college. In college, I made new friends and got involved in the mountaineering club. I started to enjoy climbing cliffs and camping in the mountains on weekends, and I was tempted by the passion. Sometimes, I would go on trips that lasted for ten or eleven days, exploring various mountainous regions, carrying a backpack with a tent for mountaineering.

First Peter 5:8–9 in the Bible reads: "Be self-controlled and alert. Your enemy the devil prowls around like a roaring lion looking for someone to devour. Resist him, standing firm in the faith." This passage is indeed a call for vigilance and spiritual preparedness. It emphasizes the need to remain steadfast in faith and to resist the devil's attempts to undermine one's faith and well-being. It encourages believers to stay self-controlled and alert in the face of spiritual challenges.

COLD FAITH

When I was in college, I failed to remain strong in faith and, instead, got caught up with my college friends in an exciting mountaineering club. I lost sight of God's word and the grace I had received.

I started living a life that made me forget about the God. This made me susceptible to the devil's test and temptations, which briefly took control of my thoughts and for a while in my life.

It is a well known fact that when created Adam and Eve, he gave them (us) free will. Free will, seen from another perspective, means the authority to make choices. It includes deciding what we want to eat, the clothes we want to wear, the people we want to meet, and the things we want to do.

Moreover, we could distinguish between good and evil in our thoughts and decide to act on them or simply let our thoughts pass. We can choose to act on godly thoughts given by God, following the guidelines mentioned in the Bible. Especially those found in religion, comprising rules that embrace the thoughts of compassion and love conveyed by Jesus in our actions, regardless of whether they seem significant or not. This would bring joy to God.

Galatians 5:19–21 (KJV) reads:

> Now the works of the flesh are manifest, which are these; Adultery, fornication, uncleanness, lasciviousness, Idolatry, witchcraft, hatred, variance, emulations, wrath, strife, seditions, heresies, Envying, murders, drunkenness, retellings, and such like: of the which I tell you before, as I have also told you in time past, that they which do such things shall not inherit the kingdom of God.

When the devil tries to seize opportunities through the works of the flesh mentioned in Galatians, I have spent years distancing myself from God and living in remorse. Today, when such sinful thoughts quietly creep into my mind, I command the devil to depart in the name of Jesus.

During living in that lifestyle without God, I met my first husband from Texas. We initially settled in Florida. Due to my husband's frequent business trips, I felt lonely in the United States with no children and no family.

I met a Korean deacon from the Korean church near the market. I began attending a small Korean church and my fading faith started to grow again, like a tiny sprout. I diligently attended the church, never missing out on Bible studies, and faithfully participated in worship services.

One of the sermons that I remember and recall now is from a special lecture on the book of Revelation that I attended. During this educational period, the pastor printed out an article from a newspaper and distributed it to the attendees, then he spoke.

Pastor: "This newspaper article is about something we need to be careful about in the last days. It talks about an invention from a research institute in the United States. They have developed a safe plastic liquid that can be injected into the human body without causing any harm or issues."

And the pastor continued with his words:

"They have already experimented by injecting this liquid into fish and it was successful. This plastic liquid can be used to insert a scannable barcode into a person's flesh."

I heard this sermon thirty-five years ago, which discussed the connection between the mark of the beast in the book of Revelation and real-world events that could potentially occur as a warning. I listened to the sermon with great impact. The pastor provided a paper with an explanation alongside a picture of fish.

BLACK AND WHITE PEOPLE IN TEXAS

My husband and I lived in different states due to our work, but it was a given that we would visit Texas, where my husband's family lives, for Thanksgiving and Christmas, which was our annual traditions. We've been to Texas several times and have become close with American couples who were my husband's elementary school classmates.

Once, during a visit to Texas, something happened. It's a small town with a population of only two thousand residents, so I, along with a Chinese family who owned a Chinese restaurant, were the only Asians around in that small town. Wherever I went, white Americans kept looking at me, young and old. Looking at me from behind or on the sly, as if they couldn't help themselves.

One day during my visit to supermarket, I was standing in line to check out items, and a cute blond-haired boy with his mom kept staring at me. I was curious about why he was so interested. Even his mom gave him a nudge to not to keep staring. But he continued to look at me in amazement. I couldn't help but smile every time our eyes met because the boy was so adorable.

The young child asked me this question:

Child: "What are you?"

Normally, we should ask people, "Who are you?" I found the question so cute that I wanted to play along, so I replied with a bit of humor:

Jennifer: "I'm an alien."

I remembered the foreigner/outsider number I used to have in my immigration status, and the word "alien" was the same. We all laughed together, and I asked the child:

Me: "How old are you?" The child held up four fingers and said he was three years old. So, we all laughed once again.

After staying in that small town, after a while, I became curious about something. So, I asked my husband.

Jennifer: "In America, there are many different races, and there are also a lot of black people, but there aren't any here, are there?"

The next day, my husband drove for a few minutes to take me to a small town. As we entered the town, we started to see Black people. They were dressed in old-fashioned attire that seemed to belong to the early 1900s, wearing faded denim overalls and hats. As our car passed by, they would take off their hats, hold them to their chests, and bow their heads to our car until we passed them. It felt truly fascinating.

My husband took me to the house that once belonged to his late uncle. It was a house that had partially burned in a fire. His uncle, who had fallen in love with a black slave woman, had built a home in this town when she couldn't enter the white community, to live with her.

I saw a picture frame in one corner that contained a picture of his late uncle and the black woman he loved. It touched my heart, and I had a bittersweet thought. His uncle must have faced disapproving glances in that region where racial discrimination was severe due to his love of the black woman. I applaud his courage in leaving the white community to live with the woman he loved.

In the past, black people had to sit in the back of the bus, were not allowed to enter white-owned restaurants, could not drink water from the same fountains in parks and cities that white people used.

And to go even further, there were designated white-only lakes, especially a lake on the vast fields owned by the state, where children came to play and swim in the summer. Black children were not allowed to go to the lake; it was for white kids only.

In other words, places that were used by white people were off-limits to black people due to racial discrimination based on differences in skin color. In the past, such discrimination was common in the southern United States, including states like Louisiana, Mississippi, Alabama, Kentucky, and more, which are located around Texas.

It reminds me of the TV miniseries *Roots* that aired in the late 1970s. It tells the story of Kunta Kinte, a young African warrior who was captured and sold into slavery in the eighteenth century America. The series depicts the harsh conditions in which he and his descendants lived and their relentless pursuit of freedom.

The town in Texas is known to be a neighborhood where only black people lived since before the American Civil War. Black residents were not allowed to enter the predominantly white areas. Even after the abolition of slavery was passed in 1833, their descendants remained isolated from white communities for over one hundred years. Some of these descendants still serve the descendants of their ancestors' white plantation owners to this day. When I visited the black town was around late 1990.

When we needed repairs or service workers came to our home, we would call the service center in the area. However, I noticed that when white workers came to fix the house, they would always bring black workers along with them.

And they let black workers do all dirty and challenging tasks only while white workers stand there to watch. Like working under the house to fix the boiler or plumbing. These types of tasks were assigned exclusively to black workers, and witnessing this discrimination made me irritated.

My husband and I were close friends with another white couple, and we often visited their home, playing card games, chatting, and spending time a lot together. During these visits. I noticed that they would make derogatory remarks about black people, crack jokes at the expense of black individuals, and laugh among themselves as if it were all in good fun. I couldn't hold back and said to them:

Jennifer: "Please stop making fun of black people! I don't want to hear those jokes!"

White friends responded to me:

White friend: "You're white, so we're just making fun jokes."

I replied to their words:

"I am absolutely, positively not White. I'm a person of color, just like black people. You folks calling me 'yellow butt Korean!!"

From then on, when they met me, they didn't make black jokes anymore. Occasionally, they showed me the Bible verses and said they prayed all the time. They told me they really love God.

Southern people in the United States, including my friends, often take pride in considering themselves devout, born-again Christians. They believe that God truly love them, and they think they have strong faith. The tendency to discriminate based on different skin colors is still deeply ingrained in their hearts.

Having lived in the United States for over thirty years, I've experienced and personally witnessed numerous instances where underlying ideas of white supremacy persist in the minds of many people in American society.

In Galatians 5:19–21, the term "divisions" refers to the act of dividing, separating, breaking unity or connection, or causing discord and differing opinions. Even animals became agitated and hostile when treated with discrimination. Any form of discrimination or division is a sin. I feel sorry and sympathetic for my friends, so I pray with the hope that they may come to know God better.

And I repent. While living in Korea and even after coming to the United States, I thought and spoke ill of people of other races and nationalities, not treating them with respect.

Jennifer: "Those people are lazy. Why do these people look so dark and ugly? They must be ignorant, coming from those poor countries!"

"Lord, I am a sinner among sinners. I humbly kneel in repentance, acknowledging my sin. Please have mercy on me and forgive me in the name of Jesus. Amen."

TRIP TO LA

While living in Florida, one day, a college friend from Los Angeles, who had immigrated to the United States following her husband, contacted me and invited me to her house. So I went there for a short visit. The initial feeling when I first arrived in LA was quite different from the beautiful and fantastic city I had seen on TV.

I went to Universal Studios and had various experiences, like trying to bend the iron bars with my two hands at the famous King Kong's prison escape and getting almost caught by the mechanical shark "Jaws" while riding a boat. I remember enjoying a seafood buffet, which was a novelty for me at the time.

I also visited the Chinese Theatre with the handprints, footprints, and signatures of famous Hollywood stars. The streets around that area were quite dirty with lots of litter, and there were many homeless people.

I found the people with strange attire and individuals with feathered headdresses and pink-dyed hair walking down the streets to be quite fascinating. What left the most impression though, wasn't the eccentrically dressed people or the handprints of the stars but the intense smell of urine and restroom odor vibrating in the air across the street from the theater, almost making me feel like I might throw up.

My friend invited me to visit them, but as my friend and husband both were working, my friend asked me if I'm interested to work for couple of weeks therefore. I had recently come to the United States, so I decided to take up an offer to work at a place operated by Korean merchants.

I agreed to work at that place though it would be a good idea to gain some experience when starting a job. The place is where T-shirts are sent to wholesale distributors serving across the United States; I would get my wages in cash.

The wholesale business was run by the owner and his wife. There was a woman who was older than me working a few years. Our tasks involved cleaning the store and preparing daily shipments of clothing orders to be packed into large boxes for delivery across the United States.

We had to quickly fill many boxes with a substantial amount of clothing before the end of the day, which left us no time for cleaning or disposing of the plastic bags received from the factory. After I had been working for a couple of days, the owner's wife began to criticize and scold me that the store had gotten messier since my arrival and she was getting frustrated with me.

I asked my coworkers there:

"Did they also criticize and scold you when you first started?"

My coworkers replied:

"Well, what they are doing to you is nothing, they did worse to me. I've worked here for several years, and there were many times I felt fed up and wanted to get out of here. But nowhere else to go so I endured it."

My coworker continued:

"You should consider yourself lucky that you can go back to your home state."

I was very uncomfortable and angry with the lady, the store owner's wife, who treat me badly because I was an employee. She would constantly criticize and give me a hard time. So, after a week, on a Friday, I told her:

"Ma'am, why do you give me such a hard time just because I'm new here? . . . I don't want to work here anymore! . . .Please calculate my weekly pay!"

And as I left that wholesale store, I made a vow to myself.

Jennifer's thoughts: "I will never work at a Korean-owned store or company in the United States from now on!"

Returning to Florida was great; I could relax and be happy. I could walk to the beach where white waves crashed just a short distance away. We could take a boat to the sea for fishing, and if you threw a net filled with a few chicken legs into the water, it was almost certain to catch many crabs.

As I walked along the dock where the boats were docked, it was fascinating to see sea lions that weren't afraid of people, coming very close, probably looking for food.

Additionally, as we drove around for a while, there were shops where you could buy the daily catch of crabs by the seashore, allowing us to enjoy delicious blue crabs.

One day, it was the first time I had to cook crabs. After purchasing fresh crabs caught on the day, as I attempted to put them into the water to boil one with the water boiling, I didn't realize these crabs had a such a strong fighting spirit to stay alive.

They clung tightly to the edges of the large pot, using their tiny claws to resist being submerged in the hot water, which made it really challenging to do. Afterward, I learned to temporarily place the crabs in the freezer, which was considered the most humane way to prepare them for cooking.

I slowly found a job, but with no experience, it took me some time to secure employment. After a while, a friend recommended me to apply for a job to a company that manufactures cables for computers and electronic products; I began working there.

The company had 80 percent employees who were Americans, and there were also multiracial individuals. While I was working there, two Korean women were hired at the company. One was five years older than me and the other was one year older, and we became friends. We started building a friendship by having lunch together and sharing various Korean dishes.

The Korean woman who was five years older wanted to become close friends with me shortly after we met, primarily because she thought of me as an elite since I had attended a college in Korea. At the time, my car was a new, relatively affordable Chrysler sedan. She admired my car and wanted to buy the exact same one. I didn't want to develop a close relationship with her but rather preferred a casual friendship. After a few months, something happened.

One day, I was working with other people in one corner of the company when a coworker came and raised her arms toward the sky and gestured for me to come quickly in the direction she pointed at. As we headed over, I noticed a large group of people gathered in a circle, watching something. When I got closer, I could see two Korean women engaged in a loud argument and shouting in Korean.

Witnessing that scene, I suddenly felt a deep sense of shame seeing Koreans fighting with each other on foreign soil. I typically have a soft-spoken and quiet tone when I speak, and I wanted to quickly put an end to the situation. I felt an urgency to resolve the matter.

Unfortunately, I had to use more forceful English words to communicate my message.

Jennifer: "Everyone shut up!!"

And I shouted again:

"Everyone scatter from here!!"

I then yelled at the American colleague who brought me to the fight:

"Why did you bring me here!!!"

As the incident concluded, the younger Korean colleague pointed at a swelling lump on her forehead and said:

"That woman picked a fight and claimed she was a gangster in Korea and wanted to show me how she could beat me up. She grabbed me by the hair and slammed my head onto this metal machine. Look at this, it's all swollen."

She started crying, the older Korean women wanted me to be her best friend. She was jealous of me being close to other Koreans. She vented her frustration on another Korean person.

I realized it might sound a bit extreme, but it could escalate into an attempted murder case. After that incident, I felt so embarrassed and ashamed I couldn't continue working at that company, so I resigned.

According to a certain scientific journal, modern advances in imaging technology allow the observation of how emotions in the mind trigger reactions in the brain. Emotions like joy, sadness, anger, envy, fear, and hatred are believed to occur in the brain's limbic system. The brain processes external stimuli into emotions and sends messages to the body for immediate responses to cope with the situation.

Therefore, jealousy acts as a stressor, affecting the body's health. When blood pressure rises due to unacknowledged emotions like jealousy, it can transform into hostility, depression, and other serious physical issues.

The Bible mentions that a peaceful heart leads to bodily health, but jealousy and envy can rot the bones. It also states that where there is jealousy and strife, there is confusion and every evil work, which accurately describes the situation I've experienced above.

> The heart at peace gives life to the body, but envy rots the bones. (Prov 14:30)

> You are still worldly. For since there is jealousy and quarreling among you, are you not worldly? Are you not acting like mere humans? (1 Cor 3:3)

> But if you harbor bitter envy and selfish ambition in your hearts, do not boast about it or deny the truth. Such "wisdom" does not come down from heaven but is earthly, unspiritual, demonic. For where you have envy and selfish ambition, there you find disorder and every evil practice. (Jas 3:14–16)

ANOTHER CAREER

I resigned from my previous job; I spent some time searching for another job by diligently scouring the newspaper advertisements daily. A contact from my American friend who knew I was looking for work got in touch with me, and she asked:

"Did you see the newspaper ad for the big company? They're recruiting."

Intrigued, I asked for more details, my friend continued:

"This company supplies parts to aerospace companies and Department of Defense. I've heard they pay better than other companies. But the catch is you must pass a test which can be quite challenging."

I decided to take the challenge and went to the recruitment location to apply. While applying, the exam proctor said the following:

"We'll send the people to school for one week with pay. You need to score at least seventy points or above in both the practical and written exams to be eligible to work for this company."

Continuing, the proctor explained further:

"That's because the Department of Defense and other aerospace companies require their approval, and they issue certifications. So, it's essential to pass the exam."

Oh my god! My heart sank, and I felt a little nervous. Back in Korea, I had a keen interest in English, even scoring a perfect score in the English section of the college entrance exam. I tried to reassure myself.

Jennifer's inner thoughts: "You've got reading and writing in English down, so you'll be fine."

I headed to the education center for the training and entered the classroom. Glancing around, I noticed there were twelve students, and I was the only Asian among them. I thought to myself:

Jennifer's inner thoughts: "This test must be really hard; I don't see any other Asians here but me."

The class began, and the teacher walked in. She was a very friendly young native English speaker. As the week of training came to an end, it was finally Friday, the moment of my destiny. The practical test was over, and it was time for the written exam. As a precaution, I took out the English Korean dictionary I had prepared and asked the teacher a question.

Jennifer: "I brought an English Korean dictionary just in case. Can I use it?"

The teacher happily agreed. The test wasn't that difficult, and I didn't need to use the dictionary. After completing the practical and written exams, the teacher revealed our scores.

Teacher: "The majority of you scored above seventy points, which is the passing score. I will start calling out the names of those who passed."

Teacher: "The person who achieved the highest score with a perfect one hundred in both the written and practical exams is [Name], and the second-highest scorer is Jennifer, who scored ninety-five on the written exam and one hundred on the practical exam."

I couldn't believe I had come in second. It was a source of pride to outperform these native English speakers, but I felt a bit disappointed to have missed a perfect score by just one question. Out of the twelve students present, only eight passed and were told to start work at the company the following week.

This company has been a major corporation since 1973, ranking twenty-seventh in the Fortune 500 magazine. When I started working there, the company provided everything needed for work, even hand lotion; the place was perfectly prepared, and the facilities were convenient and immaculate to ensure that employees could work comfortably.

While adapting to my new job, I made friends and found it rewarding. However, I sometimes felt that the company was so big and the working environment so perfect that it lacked a bit of flexibility and intimacy, which made it seem somewhat lacking in human warmth.

Having received certification from the training center for the job, I always included it in my resume, which made it easier for me to be employed in related jobs or not and accumulate more experience from it. I am thankful to God for guiding my path and leading my life.

FREE CITIZENSHIP

My husband's job situation might require us to move another country for a while, so we had to quickly apply for US citizenship to prepare for my physical safety while living in a different country. I discussed the US citizenship test with some colleagues at work, and among them, a Filipino colleague failed the test twice and warned me that it could be a difficult exam.

My husband obtained study material from someone who retired from the citizenship education center. Those materials covered various topics related to the US government, history, the constitution, and state and federal law.

For several weeks, I studied tirelessly, often listening to recorded materials on my audio device and even falling asleep with it. In other words, I studied diligently, memorizing the material to the point where I could provide precise answers during practice interview with my husband, scoring a perfect one hundred on expected test questions.

On interview day my husband and I went to the federal immigration services office located in Miami with confidence. Upon arriving at the interview location, as we walked towards the reception counter, we noticed that over fifty people were already seated waiting. Inwardly, I thought.

Jennifer: "Oh, it looks like we'll have to wait for quite some time" as we approached the counter to complete our registration.

My husband walked up to the registration counter and spoke to the staff without receiving any documentation to fill out. After a moment, a tall American gentleman wearing a sidearm came out of the office. He opened the counter door and told us to go inside. I couldn't help but feel that something was a bit unusual as we entered without completing any paperwork. I thought.

Jennifer: "Is this how US citizenship interviews are conducted?"

The armed American man escorted us to a well-lit office where a middle-aged, light-brown-haired American woman was waiting. As we entered the room, the man smiled and said:

"We absolutely have to make sure this lady gets her citizenship today!"

He even winked at the woman. She gave him a slightly annoyed look in response.

And then the interview began:

Interviewer: "Is this your correct address?"

Jennifer: "Yes."

Interviewer: "Did you come from Korea?"

Jennifer: "Yes."

Interviewer: "Have you ever used drugs or marijuana?"

Jennifer: "No."

The interviewer asked just a few brief questions and then said:

"You've passed the citizenship test. Congratulations."

I was stunned. It made me think:

Jennifer's thought: "The US also has shortcuts, huh?"

My husband hadn't told me about that beforehand. It turned out that his supervisor knew someone who held a high position in immigration, and the arrangement had been made in advance to quickly process my citizenship to go to another country.

After exhausting weeks of studying the US Constitution, history, laws—and the names of the original thirteen states—I shouted in my head, "New Hampshire, Massachusetts, Rhode Island, Connecticut, New York, New Jersey, Pennsylvania, Maryland, Delaware, Virginia, North Carolina, South Carolina, Georgia! I know these thirteen states!!"

Then I asked the interviewer:

Jennifer: "Is that all for the test? Don't you have any more questions?"

The female interviewer winked at me and said:

"Oh, I forgot to ask a question . . . what's the current president's name?"

Interviewer: "And what's the name of the governor of Florida?"

People in Florida could easily answer these questions. I passed my citizenship test quite quickly, leaving the immigration office with a bittersweet feeling. Looking back on that makes me laugh, and it feels like God might be asking me now.

God: "Jennifer, did it hurt so much to study hard about the United States? Could you have just said 'thank you' and left? Hahaha."

God is the God of love, sometimes a fearsome God, and humorous, wonderful Father God. Shortly after, my husband's overseas assignment was cancelled. Looking back, it seems like God had a different plan.

In my opinion, citizenship for inviting parents is a top priority. Therefore, God let me bring my poor mother from Korea to the United States quickly.

CHAPTER 5

Happy Life in Colorado

TO COLORADO

My husband found a new job and relocated to Colorado for a higher salary and position. We were moving to a new state with excitement and anticipation. We passed through Dallas, Texas. Until we reached Oklahoma City, there were some buildings and occasional sights along the highway.

Leaving Oklahoma City behind and driving without the end of endless cornfields and wheat fields in sight made me feel the vastness of the real America. On the first day of driving, there wasn't much to do while sitting in the car, so we snacked on potato chips and cookies, which made the journey quite boring.

As we entered Kansas, the scenery shifted to a barren, desert-like landscape, and the highway stretched on. After a while, I recalled a scene from a Western movie that was set against the backdrop of the American West during the pioneer days.

The two cowboys stood facing each other ready for a high noon gunfight. The tense music played in the background ("dun-dan, dun-dan, dun-dan"). Tumbleweed rolled, blowing through the open space between them. Tumbleweeds rolled by our car from time to time, carried by the little whirlwinds. We had been driving for a long time and I was so captivated by the landscape that I continued to gaze at it until the tumbleweed disappeared into the distance, adding an unexpected touch to our journey.

Kansas was the state where the famous characters from *The Wizard of Oz* lived. In the story, Dorothy's dog, Toto, was threatened by a wealthy woman, so they ran away and took refuge in a house that was eventually carried away by a tornado to the magical land of Oz. Passing through Kansas and thinking of the story of *The Wizard of Oz*, I felt deeply moved and filled with a sense of wonder.

Colorado is situated at an elevation of 2,100 meters, which is similar in height to Mount Halla in Jeju, with an elevation of 1,947.06 meters. The state is characterized by the Rocky Mountains that traverse it, making it the highest state in the United States in terms of average elevation. After living in Colorado for six years in a city called "One Mile High" due to its elevation, it probably would feel similar to the experience of living on top of Baekrok Lake at the peak of Mount Halla.

After spending a few days at my mother-in-law's house in Texas, we gradually drove through the gentle hills on my way to Colorado. We spent about eight hours a day driving, resting overnight at motels, and it took approximately sixteen hours to reach our destination.

In the United States, when you're driving on the highway, you'll come across rest area signs, and if you need to use the restroom, you'll need to exit there. Once you arrive at the rest area, you'll find a grassy area with just one restroom and a few benches where you can have a packed lunch.

Unlike in Korea, where you have various facilities and restaurants at rest areas, in the US, they are simple places for a quick break. After driving for a while, you may see signs for upcoming rest areas. They might say something like, "Next rest area is 150 miles ahead, so use this one." So, my husband and I, even though we didn't urgently need a break, decided to make use of the nearby rest areas, just in case.

The total distance from Texas to Colorado is 996 miles (1,602 kilometers), whereas the distance from Seoul to Gangneung is about 163 kilometers, so it's roughly ten times the distance. Colorado enjoys over three hundred days of sunny weather throughout the year.

There are times when snow can come early in the end of July and start to melt as it falls. The air and water are incredibly clean, and in the winter, driving on mountain roads can lead to the breathtaking sight of frozen snow sparkling like beautiful diamonds in the sunlight.

Colorado has clear air, and the water coming down from the Rocky Mountains is pristine and delicious. It consistently ranks in the top five states in water taste competitions each year. As you ascend the mountains, you can't help but be in awe of Colorado's stunning beauty, created by the hand of God.

When I see this beautiful Colorado, it reminds me of passages from the Bible:

> The earth is the Lord's, and everything in it, the world, and all who live in it. (Ps 24:1)
>
> From Zion, perfect in beauty, God shines forth. (Ps 50:2)
>
> O Lord, our Lord, how majestic is your name in all the earth! You have set your glory in the heavens. When I consider your heavens, the work of your fingers, the moon, and the stars, which you have set in place, what is mankind that you are mindful of them, human beings that you care for them? You have made them a little lower than the angels and crowned them with glory and honor. You made them rulers over the works of your hands; you put everything under their feet. (Ps 8:1–6)

SETTLING UP

When we arrived in Colorado driving from Texas, we stayed at a hotel called Residence Inn near the University of Colorado Boulder while waiting to find a house near my husband's workplace.

The hotel room was equipped like an apartment, including a kitchen, and we stayed there for about two months.

My husband's workplace provided us with a generous daily meal allowance, so we would dine at various restaurants in the vicinity and submit the receipts for reimbursement. For a while, exploring the different restaurants and indulging in diverse cuisines every day was quite enjoyable. However, after about a month of this routine, I started to get tired of constantly eating out once my husband returned from work.

Even though it wasn't our own money being spent, I felt that dining out was becoming monotonous. So, I decided to start cooking for us. I would purchase groceries from American grocery stores, and even though the grocery receipts were sometimes reimbursed by my husband's company, I also bought essential items within our allowed budget. I began stocking up our kitchen with groceries to the point where it filled an entire wardrobe.

After receiving several grocery receipts, my husband's company informed us that, from now on, we only needed to submit receipts for restaurant meals. As we grew tired of dining out frequently, we decided to buy groceries with our own money and cook our own meals in the hotel's kitchen.

After staying in the hotel for two months, we bought a 2,800-square-foot house located in Longmont, a city about a fifteen-minute drive north of Boulder. The house had around ten solar panels on the roof and was quite spacious for the two of us, making us feel a bit lost but comfortable.

Upon moving into the house, we noticed a collection of Celestial Seasonings herbal tea boxes neatly stacked in the kitchen and dining room. We inquired with the real estate agent about the presence of these tea boxes in the house.

It turned out that the house we had purchased was previously owned by the CEO of Celestial Seasonings, tea company. They had moved to a larger house after making a lot of money, leaving these tea boxes as a parting gift to us. That's when we began occasionally enjoying Celestial Seasonings Sleepy Time tea before bedtime.

Additionally, as winter arrived, we were astonished to find that our electricity bill, which had been around six dollars per month during the summer, had suddenly skyrocketed to sixty dollars per month. We were quite surprised by this increase. When we asked our American friends about it, they mentioned that they often paid over two hundred dollars per month in electricity bills during the winter.

I realized back then that the ten solar panels installed on one side of the roof, about the size of a window, had been generating electricity. The electricity generated was used to heat water, run the heater, power appliances, and any surplus electricity was sold back to the city, which resulted in our lower electricity bills. Since then, I became a fan of solar energy. After settling into the house, we had an opportunity to visit a friend's house.

When we visited, our friend forgot some items needed for dinner preparations and suggested that we ride together in his car to get them. I agreed to accompany them. We drove a few miles when suddenly he said it was a bit warm and decided to open the car window. In that moment, my husband and I exclaimed, "Oh my God!" Our faces turned yellow due to an indescribably strong odor of pig manure that filled the car. Our friend burst into laughter at our reaction.

After a few more minutes of driving, and now a smell worse than pig manure, a tsunami of chicken droppings odor engulfed us. Our friend, who was driving, was laughing so hard at our expense that he had tears in his eyes, and he said:

"I'm laughing so hard I think I'm going to pee on my pants!"

And then he continued:

"Whenever friends visit, it's our household tradition to bring them here as a commemoration."

Due to our friends and their peculiar tradition, whenever I think about Colorado, this memory always comes to mind. In the high-altitude, intensely sunny, and dry climate of Colorado, I had to use body lotion frequently as my skin would get very dry and flaky. Shortly after moving there, I even experienced a case of nosebleed due to the extreme dryness. Cooking required more time because water boiled more slowly at the higher altitude and baking often required adding an extra quarter cup of flour to Colorado cake mix boxes because items didn't rise as easily. The thin air also made me feel fatigued until I acclimated to the higher altitude.

Furthermore, Colorado experiences heavy snowfall in winter, but the snow is light and fluffy, making it challenging to build a snowman since the snow just scatters when you try to pack it. To engage in a snowball fight or make a snowman, you would need to spray the snow with water using a spray bottle.

FARMS AND GRAZING AREAS

Colorado is approximately half farmland, with cities like Longmont and Lafayette located east in the state, which are areas of farmland and livestock ranches. The top three grains typically grown in Colorado are corn, hay, and wheat. In the fall, you can go to a corn farm and buy around fifty ears of corn at an affordable price, blanch them, and freeze them to enjoy corn on the cob for dinner throughout the winter.

According to the Colorado Farm Bureau, the top three annual crops in terms of production are as follows:

Hay and haylage - Annual production: 1.0 billion dollars.

Corn - Annual production: 845.6 million dollars.

Wheat - Annual production: 466.1 million dollars.

Additionally, the state's largest source of income comes from cattle, with over 2.8 million head of cattle and calves, making up 66 percent of Colorado's agricultural income, totaling 7.1 billion dollars annually. Pigs also contribute significantly, with around 750,000 pigs worth approximately 136 million dollars. In addition to large cattle ranches, there are smaller farms, like the one owned by a coworker's wife in Lafayette near Longmont. They raised horses, rabbits, chickens, and pigs to feed their family. One year, they asked us if we would purchase a piglet, raise it to a certain size, and then share it with the family, both each taking half for their own consumption. They invited us to see a piglet they just purchased.

Jennifer: "This piglet is really cute and lovely . . . what if we give it a name?"

Friend: "You shouldn't think of this piglet as a pet. Giving it a name is not a good idea."

Jennifer: "Why not?"

Friend: "If you give this piglet a name, it'll start recognizing that name as its own, respond when called, and bond with you. Later on, it might become difficult for you to eat the pig."

My friend's words are true.

Forming a bond implies love for one another. I currently own two cats. My cats know their names, recognize the names of treats they like, and understand various words such as "come here," "no," and "sit." They are my children, part of my family. You can't eat your children or your family.

So, when the piglet had grown enough to be taken to the slaughterhouse, I didn't visit our friend's house to see it. When they loaded the pig onto the truck to send it to the slaughterhouse, it seemed to know, and it cried for a while, as if it understood its fate.

Luckily, since the piglet didn't have a name and didn't form a strong bond, we were able to eat the meat. When we took the pig we raised at home to a specialized butcher, they partially packaged it, made delicious smoked bacon, and the meat was much tastier than what you find at the grocery store. We enjoyed it thoroughly.

At my friend's house, their teenage son had a dream of becoming a rodeo rider, so they raised a few horses. To help me, who had never ridden a horse, their younger son placed a special saddle on the horse and assisted me in mounting. But the moment I got on the horse, it suddenly started kicking its hind legs and raised its back as if to tell me to get down.

Horses can sense the emotions of people through their skin. My fear and anxiety, trembling in my legs, made the horse uncomfortable and anxious, which is why it wanted me to dismount. I don't think I'll ever be a horse whisperer. The closest I've come to communicating with horses is when they come close for more carrots.

POPULATION DENSITY AND FOOD

The United States conducts a census (population count) once every ten years to measure how many people live in the country. According to the 2020 census statistics, the population distribution in Colorado is as follows:

According to the US Census, the population can be categorized into four major racial groups: 61.6 percent White, 18.7 percent Hispanic, 12.4 percent Black, and 6 percent Asian. The remaining 7.4 percent includes American Indian, Alaska Native, Hawaiian, and Pacific Islander populations.

According to the South Korean Ministry of Foreign Affairs in 2021, there are a total of 2,633,777 Korean residents in the United States, with 50,000 of them living in Colorado.

In the religious sector, among Colorado residents, 50 percent are Christians, 20 percent are Catholics, 3 percent are Latter-day Saints, 2 percent are Jewish, and 1 percent are Muslim, while 24 percent are non-religious. According to the 2020 US national statistics, the percentage of non-religious people is 30 percent, and if you calculate the rate at which Christians are abandoning their faith, it is predicted that by 2055, 46 percent of the population will be non-religious, according to an analysis by the US Christian Post Institute.

It's sad to see people turning away from God. We hope that this prediction does not come true. We should all earnestly pray for these individuals, the poor and unfortunate souls. It would be wonderful if these souls returned to God, and heaven could be a place of daily celebration.

In the past, when I lived in Colorado over thirty years ago, there was a small Korean grocery store in Aurora where I was fortunate enough to buy and enjoy kimchi and occasionally purchase Korean goods.

I've heard that now in Denver, the capital of Colorado, and in Aurora, there are many Korean markets, and the Korean population has increased significantly. Aurora is often referred to as the

Korean town, and even though it's a bit separate from Denver, it's considered a single metropolitan area.

To visit a Korean store, you had to drive for approximately one and a half to two hours round trip, so during the weekdays, when I occasionally craved kimchi, I would buy cabbage from American markets and make kimchi by adding spicy Mexican serrano peppers.

I personally love radishes, including various types of radish kimchi, but at that time, American markets didn't have any Asian radishes. So, I would buy round and red radishes and make a radish kimchi, but it tasted different from Korean radishes, with a spicier and slightly bitter aftertaste.

Moreover, in the new house I moved to, the previous owner had nicely set up a home garden with beautiful fences on one side. Next to it, there was a thirty-centimeter-wide, one-meter-long sand patch where an unusual plant was sprouting about fifty centimeters apart. I later learned that it was asparagus. Growing as a type of vegetable in the garden, I didn't know how to cook it when its stems were just the size of a finger. So, I simply ate it raw by dipping it in red pepper paste.

The fresh asparagus was crunchy, but it didn't have much flavor, so I didn't eat it again and just let it grow. Sometime later, I was surprised to see that the young shoots had grown into a bunch of trees. I realized that the asparagus I had eaten was from cutting down one stem of the tree-like growth, like the way bamboo shoots are harvested.

There's a folk story passed down that after eating asparagus, urine may have a strong, unpleasant odor. It's said that if anyone has unpleasantness in their urine the person might have connection with royal blood. I'm not sure it can be proven scientifically.

This odor is due to asparagus containing an acid that produces a substance like sulfur during the body's breakdown process, and when sulfur is released into the air during urination, it creates an unpleasant smell. While it's challenging to provide solid evidence, it's believed that asparagus can lead to this phenomenon in some people.

JOB SEARCHING

After moving to Colorado and a few months passed, I began to feel somewhat settled. Being at home was getting boring and monotonous, so I decided to create my resume to look for a job. I had worked in Florida and had put in a lot of effort to improve my English skills through reading, writing, and conversation, thanks to which my English proficiency had improved significantly.

I wrote a resume in English diligently, and my husband helped me correct some grammar and spelling, but more than 95 percent of it was created by me. I took my very first resume made in the United States and visited a local temporary employment agency for a job interview.

It was my turn, and a middle-aged, native English-speaking woman with blonde hair named Linda began reviewing my resume and started the interview.

Linda: "You don't have much experience listed, but it seems like there's a bit. Did you write this resume yourself?"

Jennifer: "Yes, that's right. I wrote it myself, and my husband helped with some editing."

Linda: "Hmm . . . really? I find it hard to believe that you did this yourself."

Jennifer: "It's true, I wrote it myself."

Linda: "I find it hard to believe that you did it yourself. I don't have any job to offer you."

That woman didn't trust how an Asian person had written such a well-crafted resume. It seemed like she had never encountered an Asian person who was proficient in English. She began to dismiss me and found excuses not to offer a job.

Afterward, I looked through newspaper job ads and found a position at a small American company that manufactured small components. I got the job and worked there for a few months. One day, the supervisor of the company called me into the office for a conversation.

Supervisor: "Jennifer, you've been working here as a temporary employee for a while, and you've been doing a great job. We'd like to hire you as a full-time employee."

I felt grateful for a company that recognized my skills. The supervisor continued the conversation.

Supervisor: "As a full-time employee, how much salary would you like?"

At that moment, I asked for a typical wage, adding about half of that. The supervisor thought the wage was too high for their new hires and asked me to reconsider. I explained that I couldn't accept less, and I continued working there for a while on the same wage.

One day during lunch, I saw a newspaper ad. A nearby company was expanding significantly and urgently needed to hire several employees. A few days later, after work, I submitted my resume to that company. The company's vice president personally interviewed me that same day, and I was hired. While working in another company at the new job, the company acknowledged my hard work and dedication, I was promoted to a higher position as a documentation controller. The company's office had three team leaders, who also acted as supervisors, and their desks were placed there.

One day, I entered the office with some documents to submit. While walking through, I noticed the desk of the central-left supervisor. It belonged to a middle-aged, native-born female supervisor who was responsible for overseeing the work. Suddenly, the Holy Spirit spoke to me.

Holy Spirit: "Jennifer, you will sit at that desk."

I was taken aback, thinking, "The supervisor is still working in that position, and she hasn't indicated she's leaving. How can I, with no experience, take that desk?"

A few months later, my future desk's supervisor, out of the blue, had to resign because her husband's health suddenly deteriorated, and she needed to care for him. I had been contemplating this for a while. I thought I could take on the role of supervisor at that desk, and I wanted to give it a try. After much consideration, I discussed it with my husband. He had this to say:

Husband: "If you really want this and you're eager to try, how about asking the vice president?"

Jennifer: "I really want to. Should I go and talk to him?"

Husband: "You have nothing to lose."

Jennifer: "You're right! I have nothing to lose! Even if I don't become a supervisor, I can continue going to work."

The next day, on a quiet afternoon, I went to the vice president's office.

Jennifer: "Vice President, may I ask you something?"

Vice president: "Of course, go ahead."

Jennifer: "The current supervisor will be leaving soon. Would it be possible for me to take on the role as her successor?"

The vice president was the one who had interviewed me and had given me the position of handling documents because he recognized my diligence. I had some rapport with him, so I asked without feeling overly intimidated. The vice president, who had noticed that I had no supervisory experience despite being assertive during the interview, said the following:

Vice president: "You really want to do this even though you have no supervisory experience?"

Jennifer: "Yes, I want to give it a try."

Vice President: "Alright, then start on Monday."

The vice president's words meant that he couldn't give me the official title of supervisor since I had no relevant experience. Instead, he intended to observe how I handled the tasks. It was a temporary testing opportunity, and he could revoke it at any time. After hearing this, I responded to the vice president:

Jennifer: "I can't start on Monday."

The vice president, surprised by my response, chuckled, and asked:

"Why not? What is the reason"

Jennifer: "I've been closely observing the department, and it seems like the quality of work is quite poor. I'd like a week to collect information and find solutions before I begin."

The vice president's face lit up with an approving smile as he responded.

Vice president: "Ah, that's a brilliant idea. Okay, start the job a week from now."

Afterward, I spent a week reviewing documents such as production records and quality evaluations produced by the department to identify the areas with the most issues and parts with quality problems. With this information in hand, I began my work.

As an interim supervisor, the first task I undertook was to reorganize and set up the production line for the production management section of the manufacturing department. To improve quality performance and enable mass production, I measured the time it took to assemble each product down to the second.

The production staff typically worked at their individual stations, assembling the entire product by themselves. In the new setup, we had a moving line of four people working together on a single product, dividing the assembly process into four segments with precise time allocations.

The process involved the first person completing one-fourth of the assembly and passing it to the next person, who would first inspect the quality of the previous segment. If there were no issues, they would continue with their portion and pass it on.

This relay-style moving line assembly continued until the final product was complete. The employee with the most experience would then perform a final product inspection and deliver them to the department's inspectors in sets of twenty.

This new setup not only improved efficiency and quality but also fostered camaraderie among the employees, leading to effective teamwork and trust-building. Moreover, it enabled us to manufacture a large quantity of products of high quality.

The company's workforce consisted of 90 percent white employees, with the remaining 10 percent comprising individuals from various racial backgrounds.

The achievements became known to the office managers, the vice president, and the president. Then quality managers hosted a pizza party to celebrate the fact that the department's quality had improved by 200 percent.

As I continued to produce high-quality products, I received approval for the formal supervisor position. The company started assigning me the most challenging products they had. Consequently, I managed three departments and had a busy professional life. It was fulfilling.

During my time in this role, two white women seemed to take issue with having an Asian person as their boss. They eventually approached me with the following remarks:

White woman: "Jennifer, you might see this job as a career, but to me, it's just a way to make a living, so I'm quitting!"

Jennifer: "If you quit your job, that's your choice, but is there anything I can offer you to encourage you stay with the company?"

White woman: "There's nothing you can offer me."

Subsequently, she became upset left the company in frustration. She's correct! I don't have anything to offer her because I cannot change my identity or embrace another race. I will never desire to alter who I am, as God create me this way.

THE GAZE OF DISCRIMINATION

One day at work, I noticed an American male team leader from another department struggling with assembling the basic product we were working on. When I saw he was having difficulty with the final part, I approached him and asked:

Jennifer: "May I ask you something? Shouldn't the final part be done this way?"

The male team leader, seemingly upset, responded dismissively:

"I don't want to hear what you have to say. I'll ask the engineering manager."

Jennifer: "Well, then, go ahead."

The male team leader went to inquire and returned later. I asked him:

"What did the engineering manager say?"

Male Team Leader: "He said to do whatever you tell me to."

Throughout the company, from the president to the managers, everyone trusted me. I was grateful for those who had faith in me. With the opportunities and wisdom that God provided, I was able to resolve these issues and gain recognition in the workplace. I give thanks and glory to God for everything.

One day, as I was walking down the hallway at work, I noticed a petite young American woman entering the company premises and looking somewhat lost. I approached her and asked:

"Can I help you with something?"

The young woman, with a rather condescending expression as if to say, "Who are you to interfere?" looked me up and down and then said:

"I don't know if you can help, but I'm looking for Tina, the team leader."

Jennifer: "I see. I'll let Tina know that you're looking for her. Please wait in the break room."

A few days later, the petite young American woman was hired, and we crossed paths in the hallway. She greeted me with a smile, expressing her apologies.

Young Woman: "Good morning, Jennifer. I'm working here now" (small laugh).

Jennifer: "That's wonderful! Welcome. Nice to see you again."

With that, the young woman tucked away the tail of condescension she had brandished earlier due to my being an Asian woman and headed back to her department.

In addition to this story, I'd like to share a few more instances of racial discrimination that I've experienced.

While working at the company, Halloween rolled around. I was busy with work and needed to retrieve something from my desk. On my desk, I kept various documents, clip folders, pens, and my nameplate. In one corner, there was a cute little basket filled with various candies, seemingly placed there by someone.

As I was making my way back to the office with the documents I needed, I encountered a middle-aged, American woman. I recognized her instantly, and it seemed she recognized me as well. However, she put on a forced smile and said:

Woman: "Hello. I'm Linda, from the temp agency, who left the candy on your desk."

Jennifer: "Oh, hello! I remember you. Nice to see you again."

The woman's face turned red, and she was at a loss for words. She was the same person who had initially ignored me due to being Asian when I applied for the temporary position in the office. It was quite an unexpected turn of events. She had come to plead for my help in finding temporary work for her office, the very office where she had worked when I first interviewed her.

There's an idiom: "Don't step on other people's toes, someday they will step on your toes." It means that you should be careful not to hurt, anger, or insult others' feelings, as someday, the same may happen to you.

Next, I'll share an incident that happened when I was living in Texas. I had gone to visit Louisiana, which is right next to the Texan border. While walking along the streets, my husband and I noticed an elderly man, who appeared to be in his early sixties, American. His right leg seemed amputated or severely injured, and he was sitting in a wheelchair wearing military clothing. He was gazing at people passing by from the inner side of the road. We quietly walked past him on our way.

A few seconds later, the man in the wheelchair shouted out: "Go back to your country!"

In that moment, I thought to myself:

Jennifer's thought: "Judging by his age, he doesn't seem to be a Korean War veteran, but perhaps he got injured during the Vietnam War. I'm not Vietnamese, so why is he telling me to go back to my country?"

I felt upset and momentarily angry. So, I stopped on the path, turned around to face him, and stared at him with an intense gaze, almost like a dagger, while maintaining silence for a few seconds. When he met my gaze, he was taken aback and almost fell backward. I then turned around and continued my way. During that time, I realized he must have carried deep emotional wounds.

It reminded me of a Bible verse:

As we also have forgiven our debtors. (Matt 6:12)

I forgave them in that moment, perhaps because I realized I might have done something that required forgiveness from someone, and because forgiving others can help us overcome anger, sadness, and the desire for revenge.

Forgiveness can heal the wounds in my soul, allowing me to revisit those memories without feeling the pain of those wounds once more. Those events merely live in the past and are just a small part of my life.

While living in the United States for thirty-five years, I have seen the US government make efforts to address racial discrimination through education and stringent laws, which have helped improve the situation. However, even now, there are times when I encounter people like that. During those moments, I may briefly feel anger and discomfort, but I find myself praying for them.

"God, they don't know what they are doing. Open their hearts to realize that, despite differences in skin color and appearance, they are equally blessed as your children. In Jesus's name, I pray Amen."

CHAPTER 6

Mom into USA

THE WAY TO THE US

After working for a while, I decided to invite my mother and started gathering information about it.

At the young age of thirty-nine, after losing her husband, my mother raised four children on her own. She was a lovely and unfortunate woman but was also wise, smart, and strong. It seemed like God had made it easy for me to obtain the US citizenship, and it was as if he wanted her to come to the United States to live more comfortably and experience life here.

I was able to invite my mother thanks to the immigration law that the citizenship holder is number one prioritized for bringing their parent. Not long after, she arrived in the United States. At that time, there were no direct flights from Korea or no Korean airplane flying to the United States, and my mother had to travel from Seoul to Chicago, a place where she couldn't communicate with anyone. There were no cell phones at that period, and I couldn't assist her on her way. All I could do was pray for her safe arrival and anxiously wait at home.

I remember the day my mother arrived safely, but I don't recall the specific incidents that occurred during her flight. My sister later told me about them. On the day my mother was scheduled to arrive, her flight from Chicago to Denver was delayed due to heavy snowfall in Colorado and the central United States.

My mother arrived in the United States, and it was a significant event in her life. She came wearing a somewhat uncomfortable traditional Korean dress, hanbok. The flight was delayed, and the airline provided a hotel room for two. On the plane, my mother met a friendly middle-aged Korean woman who also happened to be from Chungcheong Province, her hometown, and was wearing a hanbok.

That woman had been carrying on her head a case of strong-smelling dried squid with her. My mother expresses the smell of squid stank to high heaven, and she and my mother ended up as roommates for the night at the hotel. My mother was born and raised in the rural areas of Chungcheong Province, and her dialect was quite strong. She had moved to Seoul with my father when I was two years old.

These two Korean ladies in hanbok had never stayed in an American hotel before, so they faced a dilemma in the bathroom. They had no idea how to operate the unusual faucets and were perplexed about how to get rid of the used water because there was no drain.

They decided to seek help and opened their hotel room door, venturing into the hallway. They spotted a Caucasian man passing by and the hanbok roommate of my mother grabbed his arm and tried to pull him into their smelly room. The man was taken aback, seeing these two Asian women in strange attire attempting to kidnap him, and he nervously exclaimed:

Caucasian Man: "No! No! No!"

Hanbok lady: "Oh, come on in this way, dear." (Korean)

Caucasian Man: "Please, No! No!"

The two hanbok ladies who had dragged the man into the room and then to the bathroom were now desperately trying to communicate with the Caucasian man using their hands gestures, body language.

Hanbok lady: "How do you use this strange faucet here? We must pour water like this, and then wash our faces and throw the dirty water. There's no drain on the floor here." (Korean)

Having understood the hanbok ladies, the Caucasian man replied with an "Okay" and called for room service.

The following day, while on the plane, my mother had her eyes closed when she suddenly heard a rhythmic poking sound, "coke, coke, coke," coming from the front. (Coke sound, and meaning "poking with fingers" to Korean words.)

When she looked ahead, she saw a flight attendant walking down the aisle distributing food and people saying "coke" as she handed them some black liquids. My mother couldn't speak English, but when her turn came, she also said, "coke," and received the same black beverage, which turned out to be cola.

AMERICANS WHO EAT UNIQUELY

The next day, to celebrate my mother's first visit to the United States, we went to a nice restaurant for dinner. We all ordered steak, and it came with bread and salad. When my husband started eating his steak, my mother's face looked somewhat unpleasant.

It turned out that the steak my husband ordered was cooked "rare," with just a minute or so of searing on each side, so it had a lot of pink, blood juicy tenderness. When he dipped pieces of bread into the blood juices, it made my mother feel queasy, and she exclaimed, "Yuck."

Another thing my mother found incomprehensible about Americans was how my husband would play with the dog, and without washing his hands, he'd eat potato chips, licking his greasy dirty fingers.

Later, we took my mother out to a famous restaurant with friends. This restaurant had a Western theme, and they had a strict dress code where you had to wear jeans and cowboy boots, and wearing a suit was not allowed. At the entrance of the restaurant, they had cut ties hanging on the back wall as decoration, representing many different colors and patterns of ties.

Inside, the walls were adorned with oak wood and decorated with cowboy memorabilia, including hats, lassos, and antique items. In the center, there was a circular stage for dancing, and tables were placed on both sides and on the second floor. You could watch guests dancing while eating from the upper level. We were looking at the menu when one of our playful friends suggested:

Friend: "Jennifer, it's your mom's first time here, how about ordering Rocky Mountain oysters?"

The rest of us burst into laughter at the mischievous suggestion.

So, we ordered that dish along with some chicken gizzards, and Rocky Mountain oysters for my mom, while we ordered steaks for ourselves.

Rocky Mountain oysters, despite the name, are not oysters at all. They are a dish made from the testicles of bulls, often enjoyed by cowboys in the region near the Rocky Mountains, including Colorado, Wyoming, Montana, and more. These testicles are peeled, sliced thickly, and deep-fried to a golden crisp.

As the dishes arrived, we watched my mom's reaction with curiosity to see if she would be surprised. She was calmly enjoying her meal without any signs of being disturbed. So, I asked her:

Jennifer: "Mom, how does that round fried food taste?"

Mom: "Hmm, it's kind of like chicken and also like beef. It's tender and flavorful, quite delicious."

Jennifer: "Mom, do you know what it is? It's fried bull testicles!"

As I explained the details of the food to my mom, she responded without surprise and said it tasted good, which left us all feeling a bit disappointed because she wasn't surprised.

On another occasion, I was having lunch at my workplace, and a native coworker accidentally dropped his sandwich on the floor. He quickly picked it up and took a bite. I asked him:

Jennifer: "You dropped that on the floor. Why would you pick it up and eat it like that?"

Coworker: "Oh, it's okay. We have the five-second rule. If you pick it up and eat it within five seconds, it's fine."

Jennifer: "The five-second rule?"

In the United States, it's quite common for some people to believe that it's okay to eat food that has been dropped on the ground within five seconds. However, many find such behavior strange, especially those who consider others' saliva to be unclean.

In 2006, a US research institute conducted a study on the "five-second rule" using bologna sandwiches. The study aimed to measure the level of contamination when people pick up food from the floor within five seconds.

The results showed that five seconds is enough time for bacteria, including Salmonella, and other contaminants to adhere to the food, potentially causing symptoms such as fever, headaches, stomachaches, vomiting, and diarrhea.

Americans, known for their extensive research, expanded their investigations in 2016 to include a variety of foods like watermelon, bread, and peanut butter applied to jelly candies. They discovered that watermelon had the most bacteria transferred from the floor, while jelly candies had the least. Jelly candies were found to have the fewest bacteria due to their flat and even surfaces.

Bread, especially when peanut butter was spread on it, showed bacterial contamination like jelly candies. The research went further to determine which floor types harbored the most bacteria that could transfer to food. They dropped food on wood, tile, and carpeted floors to measure bacterial contamination.

The results indicated that carpeted floors with small flat areas had the least contamination. The research report emphasized that regardless of the food type or floor surface, five seconds is an ample time for harmful pathogens to attach to the food. Therefore, it encouraged people not to pick up and eat food that had fallen on the floor to avoid unnecessary health risks.

It's strange that Americans who engage in such practices, like eating food dropped on the floor, licking their dirty fingers, blow their noses at the eating table. Some American told me, in the past, making noises while eating, or talking, burps, may be considered rude or lacking etiquette by others.

The Korean language involves less tongue movement, less sharp and soft sounds, allowing for conversation while eating. In contrast, English often requires loud speech, wide mouth movements, and tongue involvement to pronounce words correctly.

For example, pronouncing the English words "talk or too rude" while eating can result in a rare bloody steak springing from your mouth and hitting the person in front of you, causing you to be perceived as rude and impolite. So, one should be mindful of their etiquette when speaking English while eating.

Referring to the Bible, in Gen 11:1-9, it is mentioned that at that time, people communicated using a single language and attempted to build the Tower of Babel, aspiring to reach the heavens, and become like God, falling into the temptation of Satan. To challenge the rebellion of humanity, God saw that having a common language allowed them to engage in such behaviors. Therefore, he confused their language to scatter them.

In my opinion, when examining the nuances of languages, one might wonder if God, when creating the English language, intended for people to eat in silence, bow their heads, and express gratitude for the provided food.

LIVING WITH MOM

I have a Korean habit that hasn't changed even after living in the United States for a long time. It's the practice of washing my face twice a day, in the morning and evening, which most Koreans follow, regardless of where they live.

In the United States, people typically shower every other day, but they usually skip washing their faces and only brush their teeth. Occasionally, you come across people at work with eye boogers, likely due to this practice.

It seems that in the past, Koreans used to visit public bathhouses once a week to wash their bodies, which may have given rise to the custom of washing the face. Even though modern bathrooms are available in Korea today, and people can shower anytime they want, Koreans still make sure to wash their faces in the morning and evening. As a result, Koreans are renowned for their cleanliness.

In a previously read article, a famous "D" vacuum cleaner company conducted a survey to determine which country is the best at house cleaning worldwide. The results showed that Koreans topped the list as the nation that cleans their homes the most. Koreans typically clean their houses at least twice a day, and some people even do it as many as ten times a day.

The "D" company stated that, before launching a new vacuum cleaner prototype for consumers, they conduct performance testing in Korea to allow Korean consumers to use and review the product.

This is because Koreans provide very detailed and thorough feedback on any issues, which prompts the company to address the problems and redesign the product until it achieves a satisfaction rate of over 90 percent before deciding on its release. This proves that Koreans are indeed a remarkably clean nation.

My mother, who was one of the clean members of this clean Korean nation, was exceptionally good at cleaning when she lived with me. One day, when I returned home from work, I noticed that my mother had a displeased expression.

She told me that the new vacuum cleaner, which hadn't been used for long, had malfunctioned. Upon inspecting the machine by opening its lid, we found that the motor inside had completely burnt out and melted. Looking at the charred vacuum cleaner, we talked.

Jennifer: "Mom, how much did you use the vacuum cleaner for the motor to burn out?"

Mom: "I only used it twice a day, is that too much? Is it a bad vacuum cleaner?"

Jennifer: "Mom, vacuuming once a week is enough."

Mom: "No! The carpet accumulates so much dust. I must do it every day!"

So, we ended up purchasing a better and more expensive vacuum cleaner.

Back then, it was wonderful having Mom at home. She was not just my mother but also a friend with whom I could always have interesting and enjoyable conversations. We would chat a lot and share stories like friends. The six years of living with Mom in Colorado were some of the happiest times in my life.

Particularly, when I came home from work, as Mom didn't know much about American food, she would prepare some of my favorite Korean dishes, like bean sprout soup and a few simple side dishes.

She set them on the dining table in advance, knowing that I needed to eat something before marking dinner for my husband and rest for a bit. Those simple bean sprout soups were exceptionally delicious back then. I'd gladly trade all the other luxuries in the world just to have Mom's homemade meals again.

One day, after coming home from work, Mom had something to tell me.

Mom: "I went for a neighborhood walk today, and at one house, they had some poppy flowers, so they gave me a few seeds."

Jennifer: "Mom, you don't speak English; how did you ask for them?"

Mom: "I just pointed at the flowers and said 'see, see,' and they gave me a handful."

Then I remembered something. In English, "seed" is pronounced as "see," with a strong emphasis on the first part and a weaker "d" at the end, so when you say "see" in Korean, it sounds like the English pronunciation of seeds. The Korean seed says *see*.

Jennifer: "Mom, that's used to make opium."

Mom: "That's right. When I was young and had no access to doctors in the rural areas, we would use it to make our own medicine for minor ailments."

Mom mentioned that in her childhood, people in the countryside would extract the thick white syrupy juice from the poppy plant when they made a homemade remedy; sometimes people used the whole plants as well as there were no doctors around.

She remembered happy times when she was young while looking at the poppy flowers and enjoyed growing a few plants in the front yard. In the United States, it's permitted to grow few poppies, if they are kept as ornamental plants in front yards.

After this incident, Mom asked me to teach her English. She was already mastering English alphabets, and she was soon attending an ESL (English as a second language) school to learn basic conversational English.

Mom could pronounce simple English greetings like "good morning," "how are you," and "thank you" with great precision. However, one day, after returning from ESL class, she seemed upset.

Mom: "I don't want to go to ESL school!"

Jennifer: "Why? What happened?"

Mom: "After class, they paired us up with a young Asian man, and we were supposed to practice together. While practicing, he kept telling me that I was mispronouncing 'thank you.'"

Jennifer: "Mom, your pronunciation of 'thank you' is perfect."

Mom: "That's what I told him, but this guy kept insisting that I should say 'sank you' instead."

Jennifer: "Next time, ask the teacher who's right, Mom."

After attending the class for a few times and dealing with the insistence on "sank you," Mom decided to quit the school. A few months later, she found a job at my company, where she earned money while learning practical conversational English on the job.

Mom worked diligently, vacuuming the house, growing her poppy seeds, and adapting to life in the United States. Meanwhile, I dedicated myself to my job, juggling three departments and producing products from one end of the company to the other. The relentless stream of orders meant that I often wished I had roller skates to keep up.

Orders kept pouring in, and there was hardly time to eat lunch. I had to work through the weekend from Saturday to Sunday. The long hours and stress began taking a toll on my health, and I started losing weight rapidly. Eventually, I collapsed near my desk, and everything went dark.

After that incident, I took a week off to rest and recuperate at home, eating and sleeping. I regained my strength and returned to work. I went to the vice president's office and said:

Jennifer: "Mr. Vice President, I collapsed due to overwork, but I've taken a week off and I'm back now."

Vice president: "I see. Are you feeling better?"

Jennifer: "Yes, I'm fine. I can't work on Sundays anymore. I'll only work until Saturday. If you want to terminate my employment because of this, you may."

Vice president: "Very well, from now on, you'll only work until Saturday."

At that moment, working nonstop and crossing the boundary between life and death became a reality. There was no other choice, and I left the vice president's office."

When I returned to my desk, I found that the supervisors from other departments were waiting for me. I shared the conversation I had with the vice president with them. After hearing my story, they all decided to go to the vice president's office to have the same conversation. As they left, I called out to them.

Jennifer: "Hey! Did you only have the courage to go talk to him now because I went first and told him I won't work on Sundays? Why didn't you guys ask him first?"

Colleagues: "We wanted to talk too, but we were afraid of getting fired. It was you who cut the safety tape for us to have the courage to go. Thank you, Jennifer."

THE WAY TO CHURCH

On Sundays, I started attending a small Korean church in Denver/Aurora, with about thirty congregants, thanks to an introduction from a Korean acquaintance shortly after my mom came to the United States.

I would leave home around nine in the morning, drive a long distance, attend church service, do some grocery shopping at a Korean store, and return home around four in the afternoon. Even on my one day off, my husband, who became a weekend bachelor, didn't complain about me going to church, and I was very grateful for that.

After a while, I started picking up two eighty-year-old Korean ladies from our neighborhood and took them to church with me. One of the Korean ladies was an educated woman who had graduated from EH Women's University, while the other was a simple country lady who had never even finished elementary school and lived with her husband in a small one-room apartment. On the way to church, these two ladies would often argue and bicker in the backseat, which always made me laugh.

One Sunday, while driving to church, the country lady mentioned that her husband had severe constipation, and she had bought medicine from an American pharmacy the day before. I was curious about how she managed to get the medicine when she couldn't read or speak English, so I sneaked a peek.

Jennifer: "You find English difficult, so how did you ask for constipation medicine?"

Country lady: "Oh, it's easy! I talk to the pharmacy assistant and squat on the floor making straining sounds like, 'groan' while saying, 'no dung [Korean], no dung [Korean],' pointed to my bum. That's all I did."

The educated lady shook her head in disbelief, considering it unsophisticated, and my mom and I in the front seats couldn't help but laugh so loud.

A little while later, on a Sunday when we were driving to church, we witnessed a minor fender bender involving two cars on the four-lane highway heading south towards Denver, just before the midpoint.

We stopped briefly to see if they needed help, and it turned out to be a Korean elderly couple. I approached them, thinking they might need assistance. A few minutes later, the police arrived, and we, including me, started explaining the situation to the officer, who had come to offer help.

Officer: "Jennifer, if an interpreter comes from Denver, you'd have to wait here for at least two hours. Thank you for stopping on your way to church to help. We really appreciate it."

Jennifer: "You're welcome. I'm glad I could assist because they're Korean."

With that, I began interpreting. The elderly Korean man explained that he had rear-ended the car in front of him because the car had suddenly and repeatedly hit the brakes. The officer conveyed to the elderly man that it was the fault of the car in the back for not maintaining a reasonable legal distance. The elderly man repeatedly insisted that it wasn't his fault, his frustration causing tears to well up.

Once the accident investigation concluded, I returned to my car, intending to continue to church. As I was about to drive away, the police officer raised his left hand, signaling me to stop. Confused but compliant, I waited in my car. The officer walked onto the four-lane highway, stopping all southbound traffic from the northbound direction.

And then, in front of the halted line of cars, he signaled for me to join the highway and initiated a military salute toward our car. We gradually merged onto the four-lane highway, and as we safely entered the freeway, the officer continued to salute our car. Watching this, those of us in the car, who had come to the United States, found it remarkable and novel to receive a salute from a police officer.

When we arrived at the church, the service had already begun. We entered the church quietly and tried to take our seats in the back. As soon as we walked into the church, the congregation stood up and clapped vigorously upon seeing us. Our group was taken aback by this warm welcome and wondered why everyone was so excited. I felt like I was in a surprise show.

Then, the pastor spoke.

Pastor: "One of the church members saw your car stopped on the highway due to an accident; she asked all of us to pray for you and we prayed for your safe arrival before we started the worship. You have arrived here safely, and we thank God. Hallelujah!"

Receiving this enthusiastic welcome at church was both surprising and heartwarming, and we felt grateful to have been able to help a fellow Samaritan and to offer comfort to the elderly gentleman involved in the accident. This experience allowed us to see the true principles of compassionate action as outlined in the Bible.

> And he also went on to say to the one who had invited him, "When you give a luncheon or a dinner, do not invite your friends or your brothers or your relatives or rich neighbors, otherwise they may also invite you in return and that will be your repayment. But when you give a reception, invite the poor, the crippled, the lame, the blind, and you will be blessed, since they do not have the means to repay you; for you will be repaid at the resurrection of the righteous." (Luke 14:12–14)

The elderly lady from our church, who couldn't speak English, seemed to have a keen mind. She would take the bus on her own and visit the nearby American market while taking care of her husband, who suffered from various illnesses.

Once, in the fall, the country lady suggested that we gather acorns to make some food. We went to a house that was uninhabited according to the country lady. In front of the house, there was a big acorn tree, and a substantial number of acorns had fallen and covered the grass. We brought plastic bags with us, and the three of us crawled on the ground, gathering several bags of acorns.

I wonder how much time had passed. A middle-aged, blond American lady got out of her car and silently walked past us while we were on the knees crawling. She followed the middle of the cement path that led into the house. I felt bad for picking acorns in her yard without permission, believing the country lady's words. So, I told the country lady:

Jennifer: "Lady, this is someone else's house, and the owner just walked in!"

Country lady: "Huh? I've been walking by here several times during the day and haven't seen anyone."

Jennifer: "Maybe you didn't see them because they were at work."

With worries about what the homeowner might say, I knocked on the front door. A lady with a smiling face came out, and I said to her:

"I'm really sorry for picking acorns without permission when you weren't home."

Homeowner: "Oh no, it's okay. The tree produces too many acorns, and I can't even mow the lawn because it's grown so big. In the fall, they're a real headache. They keep bouncing around the yard and even hit the car parked out front. Feel free to come by and take as many as you want anytime."

Although I felt apologetic, I came back home with the acorns after hearing the kind words of the friendly acorn homeowner. My resourceful mom, considering the dry weather, quickly spread out the acorns for easy drying in the garage.

She put a large plastic sheet on the ground and had me drive my car back and forth over it a few times to help remove the shell of acorns, which reduced the time for the process to make acorn jelly. Then, after church service and during the fellowship time, we brought them to share with the church community.

Even now, Korean people in the United States enjoy acorn jelly as a side dish. When fall arrives, families and even golf courses in the area cut their lawns, gather acorns, and put them in one place for Korean individuals to pick up. Koreans take these acorns to their gatherings and share them during regional worship services, which might seem strange to non-Korean individuals.

Korean kimchi, which is famous worldwide, has a distinct smell that some people find unappealing. However, it's a beloved dish among Koreans. Similarly, sauerkraut, a fermented food from Germany, is loved by some and might be considered peculiar by others, just like kimchi.

CHAPTER 7

Back to Hometown

BACK TO TEXAS

After living in Colorado for six years, my husband decided to take a temporary leave of absence and move back to Texas, as he felt that his current job wasn't aligning with his interests and skills. I was content with my job, but I agreed to follow my husband to Texas, as I also thought it was a good idea for both of us to take a short break.

We purchased a small house near a private lake in a neighborhood not far from my mother-in-law's place in Texas. The houses by the lake were built for private vacation purposes, and our house was one of the six on one side of the lake. The residents included our family, a couple who were my husband's elementary school friends, and a retired male school principal who was openly gay.

On the other side of the houses, it was decided by the lake's residents to leave the area untouched to allow for natural wildlife habitat. It was designated as a natural conservation area, and from our backyard, we could see large and dense oak trees.

For a while, with nothing much to do, we enjoyed the tranquility of the peaceful lake, where we would relax at home, work in our small garden, and sleep in late. It was a great time to rest and unwind.

As the evening grew dark, the howling of wolves would pierce through the sounds of crickets and insects. Unauthorized entry by non-residents was strictly prohibited around the private lakes, and illegal trespassers would be swiftly arrested if reported to the police.

The lake, not much larger than an entire American shopping mall, was perpetually fed by underground springs and never ran dry. The water continued to flow out of one end.

One morning, as I stepped out to the back porch and looked at the lake, I noticed something floating in the middle of the lake. Drifting closer due to the wind, I realized it was a beaver, an animal with four legs paddling toward the sky, floating on the water's surface. The beaver, which had been shot with a rifle the previous night from a distant location and had not yet been retrieved, was floating on the water.

It turned out that this beaver had been removed from the lake by the lake caretaker, who also happened to be my husband's friend and neighbor at the lake. The beaver had built a dam in the lake, blocking the water passage through which the spring water flowed out. This would have raised the water level in the lake and potentially threatened the houses. Unfortunately, the beaver had chosen the wrong place to build its home and met an early end.

The place we had moved to in Texas was a small, remote city with a population of about two thousand residents. It was located approximately two hours to the east of Dallas. Within the city, there were just a few small stores, a Walmart, and a handful of restaurants. If you wanted to do Christmas shopping or buy other goods, you had to drive for forty-five minutes to a slightly larger city.

TEXAS CUISINE AND INSECTS

Sometime after my husband and I moved to Texas, his elder brother, who was a senior executive at a major oil company, invited us to go on a trip to a deer hunting ranch that the company managed. That hunting ranch spanned one hundred acres, enclosed by a fence, where deer roamed freely. It was a place where company employees could apply to use for hunting.

Upon our arrival, we found a motel-like accommodation with five guest rooms and a dining area, and the trip was scheduled for three nights and four days. While the husbands were out hunting, the wives prepared meals, chatted, and anxiously awaited their return with hopes of a successful hunt.

On the first day, the husbands returned to the accommodation empty-handed, having had no success in hunting. The following day, they finally returned jubilantly with a deer they had successfully hunted.

When they returned, the men began field dressing the deer at a large tree in front of the accommodation, using a knife to cut into the deer's stiff muscles and joints. It was fascinating to witness the field dressing process for the first time, but the sight of the deer, shot by a rifle just a few hours ago, emitting steam while being disassembled, was somewhat unsettling.

After the flood, God told Noah and his family, "Every moving thing that lives shall be food for you. And as I gave you the green plants, I give you everything" (Gen 9:3), granting people permission to eat meat and have dominion over the animals he created. However, I couldn't help feeling compassion and pity for these animals, who were made by God for his people to consume.

After the hunting trip, I prepared the deer meat we brought home by tenderizing it with a meat mallet, soaking it in milk for a while to remove the blood, and then seasoning it with salt and pepper before coating it with flour and egg for frying. It's a dish that Texans typically make with beef, and strangely enough, they call it "chicken-fried steak." Instead of beef, I used deer meat to prepare chicken-fried steak. My husband enjoyed it with buttered corn and mashed potatoes. However, the gamey flavor, which is hard to describe, left an unpleasant taste for me as wild game meat tends to have a stronger and more distinctive taste.

Texans have a fondness for fried meats like chicken and beef, as well as barbecue dishes. They also enjoy frying vegetables, and one such vegetable is okra. Okra is often prepared by frying, in addition to being cooked in water. It is believed to have spread widely in the southern United States through the African Americans who migrated there from West Africa.

Okra has a taste reminiscent of grass or hay, a shape resembling a pepper, and tiny seeds inside that pop when you bite into them. The entire surface of okra is covered with small, fuzzy hairs. When cooking it in water, it needs to be blanched for just a few seconds. Overcooking okra can result in a slimy and unappetizing texture, along with a rather bland taste. Personally, I'm not a fan of okra for these reasons.

Sometime after the trip, I decided to expand the backyard garden with my mom, and while moving some stones around, I got bitten by fire ants on my right ring finger. Within minutes, my right hand began to swell up as if someone had inflated it with air, causing all the creases and wrinkles in my hand to disappear, and the swelling extended all the way to my wrist.

Looking at my swollen and tight hand, I started feeling frightened throughout my body. My husband quickly rushed to the pharmacy to get antihistamines, which are drugs that suppress allergic reactions caused by the body's response to antigens and antibodies.

After taking the medication the swelling in my hand gradually subsided. For the first time in my life, I was amazed and so happy to see thick wrinkles return to a part of my body.

The Texas region where I lived was near Dallas, and summers there were very humid, typically lasting for about three months. The average high temperature was around 36°C, and the low temperature was approximately 25°C. Winters had an average temperature of 14°C, with little to no snowfall. Texas, especially in the central and southern areas, frequently experiences large and small tornadoes due to the hot and humid conditions.

I've always tended to attract bug bites, perhaps because of my naturally warm body. And to these bugs, I'm a walking incense pot emitting a very delicious smell. One summer during middle school, I went to visit my grandmother in the countryside. After arriving, I spent one night there, and when I woke up and rubbed my eyes, my sister, who had slept next to me, was startled, and said:

"Oh my goodness! You've been bitten by mosquitoes so many times in only one night! Let me count . . . one, two, three, four, five . . . 130 times!"

While my sister was counting the mosquito bites on my body, I was busy scratching and putting my saliva to the itchy bites for relief.

The scorching hot weather in Texas means that there are plenty of insects, some of which can be real nuisances. My arch-nemeses, the bugs that relentlessly bite and feed on my blood, include the dreaded fire ants, ticks, and fleas.

Fire ants are different from other ant species, as they build mounds of dirt on the ground, some reaching heights of fifty centimeters or more. Even though I've been bitten only a few times, the swelling and pain were so severe that it felt like a major ordeal.

Fortunately, I was able to treat them promptly and didn't develop large pustules. However, I've seen a tragic story on Texas news about a young child, aged two or three, who accidentally fell into a fire ant mound and tragically lost his life. The venom in fire ant stings contains a substance called Solen opsin, which can slow down heartbeats and even cause paralysis.

Next on the list is ticks, which can transmit Lyme disease. These insects burrow under the skin of humans or animals, burying about two-thirds of their body, and reside with their back end sticking out, continuously feeding on blood. They are vicious bloodsuckers and can cause serious health issues.

The way to remove them is to gently pull them out without squeezing or crushing the insect. This method can be effective, but it can be quite challenging to execute. The most effective method I've encountered involves letting the insect experience the scorching heat of hell's inferno. By using a lighter to apply heat to tick's butt for a moment, it prompts the tick to retreat and detach itself, finding the rising temperature too uncomfortable to endure.

Lastly, there are fleas. Getting bitten by a flea is much itchier than getting bitten by a mosquito. The itching can persist for several days, even if you apply anti-itch creams or medications. If I had to choose the most annoying and itch-inducing insect bite I've experienced in my lifetime, without a doubt, flea is the most monstrous itching insect that I have known.

Even when the skin where they bit starts to heal, it continues to itch, and the welts can stay visible on your skin for years. I still have bite marks on my legs after over twenty years. Fleas are world champions when it comes to jumping. They can jump more than sixty-six times their body length, exceeding twenty centimeters. The current record for the farthest flea jump is held by a rat flea, which leaped thirty-three centimeters during a flea-jumping competition in California in 1910.

SOLITUDE

During my time in that small Texas town, I didn't meet anyone except for my mom who moved with us. Whenever I ventured outside, I felt uncomfortable under the gaze of the American people, both children and adults. People's natural curiosity towards foreigners often leads them to stare so much, which makes me very uncomfortable.

As a result, I didn't attend an American church, and I kept reminiscing about the happier times we had in Colorado, which started to torment me. I longed to return to Colorado, even if it meant going back alone.

My husband, being in his hometown, had some friends to meet, so he often came home late, and sometimes he even arrived in the early hours of the morning.

As time passed and I gazed out at the lake from the back porch, tears began to flow uncontrollably. Loneliness was overwhelming in that place, and I felt like I was the only one experiencing it. At some point, I felt bad for Mom living in such isolated places, so I asked her to go back to Korea and stay for a while, so she left for Korea.

At that time, I was in my early thirties. People need to interact with one another and form relationships, influencing each other positively. So, especially at a young age, people should help each other improve self-development and adaptability, elevating each other and growing together.

My husband would see me crying while I gazed at the lake all the time, and he told me that I made him sad whenever he looked at me. I did feel lonely, but more than being sad, I just felt down, and tears would come. I would often think that something was wrong with me and that I should see a doctor. I was beginning to experience depression, and it was getting worse.

Once, my husband received a call from the company where he had submitted his resume and wanted to talk. He was always out meeting friends, so he wasn't at home. I drove around looking for him but couldn't find him anywhere.

Since it was a very small town with not many places to go, I found it strange that I couldn't locate my husband. The next day, my husband, who had received the call from the job he was looking for, blamed me for not being able to find him. He said he was at a friend's house and lost track of time.

The house by the lake had windows connecting the entire kitchen to the living room, so when I sat on the couch, I could see the entire lake. I continued to neglect housework, barely eating, and spent my days feeling lonely, just staring at the lake from the living room.

One evening, while crying and feeling low, I remembered the Lord's Prayer that Jesus taught and started reciting it. Gradually, as time passed, I wanted to read the Bible, so I memorized the Lord's Prayer and started reading a few chapters of the Bible before falling asleep.

REBORN IN SEATTLE

As time passed, I received a call from a college friend who lived in LA. The sound of a fellow Korean's voice on the other end of the phone, especially my friend's voice, felt like a refreshing minty breeze surrounding me, making me incredibly happy.

My friend had moved to the Seattle area in Washington, and she offered to send me a plane ticket to come for a short visit. So, she sent me a plane ticket to Washington, along with an open return ticket, allowing me to visit Washington for a while.

Upon arrival at the Seattle airport, as I stepped out of the airport and onto the road, I felt the cool and clean air, a stark contrast to the hot and humid Texas weather. Washington State felt like the entire state was air conditioned, which was a refreshing change and something I truly appreciated.

The following morning in Seattle was incredibly refreshing. I headed down to the backyard of my friend's house to enjoy my morning coffee while lounging in the garden chair, savoring the fresh air. The dense fog that hung like a curtain in the middle of the Douglas fir forest, visible across from me, looked truly beautiful.

Washington State, a known as the Evergreen State, is covered in lush greenery all year round, with blue spruce, pine, and Colorado spruce trees, resembling Christmas trees. It's a place where you can appreciate the beauty of nature.

Furthermore, although Washington has all four seasons, even during the brief and warm summer, it's not overly humid. Finding shade provides a refreshing respite from the heat. This may explain why many Washington residents don't have air conditioning in their homes and instead rely on large fans during the summer.

Winters are characterized by infrequent snowfall, with only a few days of sub-zero temperatures. With mountains to the right and the Pacific Ocean to the left, there are plenty of opportunities for relaxation and recreation, making it an ideal destination for extended vacations.

My friend's place was a mid-size town just a few minutes away from American shopping malls, and you could drive a short distance to find Korean stores. There, I didn't encounter many people staring at me, which made me feel comfortable. I enjoyed going to Korean restaurants and shopping with my friend, which made me feel happy and content.

However, as a few weeks passed at my friend's house, I started feeling a sense of guilt about not returning to Texas and wondered what I was doing there. At times, my heart felt heavy.

One day, when my friend went to work and I was alone, cleaning the house hastily, I ascended the stairs to my upstairs room. In the middle of the staircase, the Holy Spirit touched my heart and spoke to me in Korean and English, in a dignified yet gentle manner.

Holy Spirit: "I brought you up here. I brought you up here" (Korean).

Hearing the voice of the Holy Spirit, I sat down right there and cried profusely. It was my God who, knowing my loneliness in Texas, saw me, comforted me, and embraced me when I shed tears, and through a friend who hadn't been in touch, brought me to Washington

A few days after this incident, I received a call from my husband's friend's wife, who was also my friend, Cathy.

Jennifer: "Hey, it's been so long . . . what's up? Have you tried calling me?"

Cathy: "Jennifer! Why haven't you come back, and what are you doing there?"

Jennifer: "Why? What's going on?"

Cathy: "Your husband cheated on you with his former high school girlfriend from the next neighborhood! Come back to Texas soon!"

That's when it hit me. It was the reason why, when my husband received calls from his new job in Texas, and I tried to reach him by driving around the neighborhood, I couldn't find him. It was because I am not that kind of person, I hadn't suspected him of having an affair.

The next day, I called my husband to find out if what Cathy had said was true.

Jennifer: "Cathy mentioned yesterday that you cheated. Is it true? Yes or no, answer me."

Husband: "Then I guess I have to say yes."

Jennifer: "You've broken the sacred trust between us as a couple . . . So, the reason I couldn't find you when I was trying to deliver a message earlier by driving around the neighborhood was because you were with that woman from the next neighborhood, right?"

Husband: "Yes."

Jennifer: "I can forgive anything else, but I can't forgive adultery! I can't trust you anymore, and we can't live under the same roof. God also allows divorce for that reason."

The betrayal by my husband and the thought of separation became a jumble in my head, and my heart began to ache, tears streaming down my face. From the other side, my husband asked why I was crying. I told him it was because I now had to say goodbye as it was time for us to part ways.

> I tell you that anyone who divorces his wife, except for sexual immorality, and marries another woman commits adultery. (Matt 19:9)

In a previous reading of an article by a pastor, I learned that the biblical basis for divorce is when a husband discovers something shameful or disgraceful about his wife. The word "shameful" in its original meaning refers to "nakedness, exposure, obscenity, immoral acts," and so on. It signifies that what is shameful pertains to indecency and abhorrent, repulsive things.

In my understanding, I realized that events connected to adultery could also be grounds for divorce. It's important to note that saying one should get divorced just because there has been infidelity is not the message here. It's a matter of choice for the individuals involved, to forgive their spouse, seek God's guidance, and, if they decide, personally reconcile, and continue to live together.

My husband's infidelity led to our divorce, but in my heart, there was an insurmountable guilt that perhaps the divorce was my fault. Afterward, I sought to understand the differences in thinking between men and women and the disparities in our communication. To address these issues, I purchased a self-help book that clearly outlined solutions and explanations. The book I selected was authored by John Gray, a couple's counselor and writer, and I read it cover to cover ten times.

At my workplace, I inquired with my colleagues about the book's descriptions of men's thoughts, and it turned out the content in the book was indeed true. Through this book, I learned a lot about the differing perspectives of men and women and discovered that our conversations as a couple often involved many self-serving thoughts, which we were unaware of. I also realized that the divorce wasn't my fault. Following the divorce, I returned to God and was reborn in Seattle.

SETTLING UP

I really like Colorado, but I have come to appreciate Seattle as well. The weather, the abundance of trees, and the frequent rain didn't make me sleepless in Seattle; instead I feel refreshed by clean air when it rains and fell in love with this place. After my divorce, I settled here in Washington. Initially, finding a job related to my career wasn't easy, so I took a temporary position at an American company that produced instant cup noodles.

At this job, I worked in the evening shift, ensuring that the cups coming out of the rotating machine, like cup ramen, were quickly packed into boxes. I had to stand and work continuously to avoid spillage.

Despite being thin and not particularly strong, I often felt extremely tired by the time my shift ended, to the point where the sky looked yellow when driving home, and I even fell asleep while driving to my friend's house.

I remembered the days when I used to be a supervisor in Colorado, and the physical and mental challenges of my current job. After saving up some money, II eventually transitioned to my own apartment. During that period, numerous individuals in my neighborhood did not possess basic early computer models.

However, there was a Japanese company nearby that produced premium high-priced laptop computers, and I was hired as an evening shift inspector. I was the only inspector in the evening shift, and most of the workers there were native English speakers, with only a few people from diverse backgrounds. I worked alone at a desk installed in the corner outside of the delivery area and the door.

The job I was doing involved inspecting completed products at the company before they were picked up by delivery trucks in the morning. Once the delivery preparation was completed, I would enter the delivery area and examine around sixty computers, all wrapped in plastic and neatly stacked in pallets.

Next, I would use a knife to cut open the plastic, and I would randomly select three computers from the top and bottom. This product quality inspection was much like a customer testing the products: checking for functionality, appearance, company logos, stickers, and so on, and then reporting the results to the managers who would come in the morning.

When I inspected the laptops from the batch, often around 90 percent of them had issues like malfunctions, damage, or problems with stickers. This meant that the products had to be separated again for further processing in the production area. It was frustrating because it wasn't the fault of the delivery department employees, yet they had to do the repacking. I couldn't help but feel resentment.

During the moments of free time in between inspections, I would listen to hymns and read the Bible on my laptop. After working there for a while, the native English-speaking colleagues in the delivery department started teasing me, calling me a crazy Jesus freak. When I entered the workplace, they would stand behind me, talking loudly and making fun of me.

Moreover, when I was in the delivery area, they would intentionally play unpleasant music and songs. They teased me every day, labeling me as a Jesus freak. Despite the persecution, I never retaliated and just quietly continued working. I would even offer words of encouragement when the products passed the inspection, and I would help without saying a word when they needed assistance. Mostly, I prayed for them.

After a few months, on a Monday, a young native employee with short hair, who had been the most antagonistic toward me, approached with a smile and said:

"Jennifer, I'm really sorry for teasing you and calling you a Jesus freak."

I replied, "I accept your apology. Thank you. But what happened?"

The young employee continued:

"On Friday after work, I went to a bar with some friends and drank until closing time. Then, as I was walking to the parking lot, I suddenly saw a scary gray cloud-like figure that appeared out of nowhere. It started screaming at me, 'You are the devil tormenting Jennifer! You are Devil!'"

I inquired, "Are you serious?"

The young employee replied, "Yes, I'm serious. I saw it, and it was terrifying. I was so scared that my heart was pounding, and I couldn't sleep that night."

The young delivery person finished sharing his story with me and returned to the delivery department, where he told his colleagues about his experience.

> So, the Lord Almighty, the God of Israel, declares: "I will punish my enemies and avenge myself." (Isa 1:24)

In the book of Romans, there are instructions from God about vengeance:

> If your enemy is hungry, feed him; if he is thirsty, give him something to drink. In doing this, you will hear burning coals on his head. (Rom 12:20)

I wonder if the Korean proverb "Give an extra rice cake to the one you dislike" might be influenced based on these biblical teachings. After all, even our enemies have consciences and know the impact of their actions.

In a sermon by a pastor, I heard that these verses from the Bible are about using acts of kindness and goodness to shame and convict the conscience of those who wrong us, like placing burning coals on their heads.

My loving God sent an angel to help me, and watching over me.

> For I am with you, and no one is going to attack and harm you, because I have many people in this city. (Acts 18:10)

> So do not fear, for I am with you; do not be dismayed, for I am your God. I will strengthen you and help you; I will uphold you with my righteous right hand. (Isa 41:10)

After the incident with the delivery person, I developed a better relationship with my colleagues in the delivery department. My work as an inspector became easier, and the production supervisor who used to pass my desk without saying much noticed my dedication. This supervisor, who worked in the production department, eventually appointed me as the team leader for the morning shift.

My leadership philosophy was not about giving orders but rather leading by example, working hard, respecting their opinions, and fostering teamwork. On one occasion, our supervisor informed me that we needed to increase production by a full shift due to a high volume of orders. As a reward, he promised to buy us pizza for lunch. I gathered my team for a brief meeting.

Jennifer: "Team, we have a high volume of orders, and we need to increase production by a full shift."

Jennifer: "If we finish making that quantity by the end of this week, we'll get pizza for lunch. What do you say, want to give it a try?"

Team members: "Sure! We can do it. Let's have pizza!"

Everyone returned to their workstations, applauding, and worked hard, all striving together to meet the increased production goal. As a result of this collaborative effort, we successfully reached our production target. Of course, everyone was delighted, and we enjoyed a pizza lunch, making those months quite fulfilling.

One day, I couldn't prepare my lunch, so I went to the lunchroom to see if there was any food left in the vending machines. While passing by a table, I saw an Asian woman whom I had seen a few times before, eating her lunch alone. Whenever I had seen her in the lunchroom previously, she was always quietly eating alone. So, I approached her and started a conversation in English.

Jennifer: "Hello, may I sit here?"

Asian woman: "Yes, you can sit here."

Jennifer: "My name is Jennifer. Nice to meet you."

Asian woman: "Nice to meet you too. My name is Esther."

Jennifer: "I'm Korean. Where are you from?"

I thought she was from another East Asian country and continued the conversation in English. Esther explained that she is also Korean and had learned English after a major accident that nearly took her life. She was living alone, and I invited her to my home for a meal, and she reciprocated by inviting me to her place. We gradually became friends, spending time together and sharing our life stories.

(Esther had a near-death experience due to a major accident. I received her permission to write her testimony in a book, and it was published in a Korean Christian magazine distributed to Korean churches nationwide. I decided to include Esther's story again in a later chapter.)

After working at the laptop company for several years, one day, the company informed employees that they would be closing the Washington State office and relocating to California. People began searching for new jobs due to the impending closure of the workplace.

One day, the supervisor at the company I worked for informed us that a company near the Microsoft headquarters, which was about an hour and a half from where I lived, was recruiting employees. With a recommendation letter from the supervisor, I and a total of ten employees went for interviews at that prospective company.

Out of the ten people interviewed, both I and another department's team leader were selected for positions in that company.

CHAPTER 8

New Opportunity

HIRED AT A NEW COMPANY

The new job I was hired for was with an American corporation located near the Microsoft campus. This company specialized in producing large-scale storage drives used by various American film studios, including Disney, for storing their movies and records due to their high capacity. They also sold their products to other companies, including Dell and IBM, who rebranded them with their logos (OEM production).

The workplace had about 80 percent native English speakers and around 20 percent employees from diverse cultural backgrounds. When I arrived at work, even though I had been hired as a team leader, I wasn't immediately assigned to a team to lead.

One of my initial tasks was to go to a subcontractor located to the north to conduct the final inspection for a batch of products until the order quantity was fulfilled. This meant spending an entire day at the subcontractor's location, I would do the final inspection before they sent their products to my company.

At that place, the products brought in by the supervisor were mostly of good quality, but a few defective ones were occasionally found. The employees at the subcontractor's location would give me icy stares that felt as cold as the chill of February. I worked beside them while feeling the cold shoulders' breeze chill my bones.

I spent several months going back and forth, commuting from work, returning to my company to write a report on the inspection results and the quantity of items to be rejected daily to the inspection department manager. Then, the time for the company's semi-annual performance review came. One day during that period, a former team leader, who was originally from the previous company with me, approached me.

Former team leader: "Jennifer, I'm in the middle of a review meeting right now, but how on earth can you get an excellent score, the highest score possible? I'm so envious."

Jennifer: "I just did the tasks as assigned to me."

Performance reviews in the United States typically use a five-level scoring system. It's a process conducted annually or quarterly, designed to set the direction for the following year's performance and execution. It evaluates past job performance, assigns appropriate compensation, and provides opportunities for promotions through company processes.

The usual five review settings are unsatisfactory, need improvement, meet expectations, exceed expectations, and outstanding, which correspond to scores given as one, two, three, four, and five, respectively. According to the former team leader, I received a score of six, which is "excellent," in my performance review.

MY DEPARTMENT

After that, I was employed as a team leader and was assigned to a department where I could begin working. This department produced their own products, and soon after, we received orders for IBM subcontracted production. As the order volume continued to increase, one day my immediate manager called me into his office.

Manager: "Jennifer, we've received IBM orders that are more than twice our usual volume. Can you think of any ideas on how to meet this quantity?"

Jennifer: "Yes, I'll think deeply and try my best to come up with a solution."

After the conversation with the manager, I went to my desk and pondered the issue carefully. Our company's product featured a deep ivory color with a bright company logo in the upper left corner, while IBM's product had a pastel black color with a silver logo in the upper right corner.

Since the internal mechanics of the machines didn't need modification, the manufacturing process wasn't particularly complicated. However, what we needed was twice the space to produce the IBM products. Then I visited the production department to measure and assess if the current space could accommodate double the production.

The result of the assessment gave me the confidence that by dividing the current production area into two equal sections and aligning them in the same direction, we could indeed produce IBM products effectively. Late into that afternoon, my team and I relocated and rearranged the production stations, installed two rows of production stations, and began producing high-quality products from the next day.

Due to the number of IBM orders, all the managers were quite tense. I was producing IBM products and had been using the functions of Microsoft Office, creating production reports in Excel that contained information about past, present, and future production quantities and quality passes.

In the morning, I handed these reports to the managers or left them on their desks. The managers appreciated the daily reports they received in the morning and found them very helpful during their meetings with their superiors.

As I passed by the shipping department, I couldn't help but smile when I saw my "child-like" IBM products piled high in various pallets, awaiting their delivery dates. Since I often had to pass by the shipping department in the course of my daily work, I noticed that one day a male coworker greeted me with a bright smile.

Male coworker: "Oh, Jennifer, hi! How are you?"

Jennifer: "Oh, hi! Hello . . . I'm good."

It was nice to receive a friendly greeting from a coworker, but I couldn't help but feel that he repeated the same routine each day as I passed by. He would energetically greet me, give me a thumbs-up, and watch me closely. So, one day, I decided to ask him about it.

Jennifer: "Greeting is nice, but why do you say hello so many times in a single day?"

Male coworker: "Uh, well . . . um."

After that brief exchange, I continued to my department to carry out my tasks. The next day, the male coworker didn't show up for work. So, I asked another coworker from the shipping department about it.

Shipping department coworker: "Jennifer, the truth is, that coworker was on a temporary assignment and had only recently joined. He didn't know you were the team leader here. When I told him that you were the team leader and that he had been too rude, he got embarrassed and decided to quit."

It seems that this coworker had a positive impression of me, seeing that I was an Asian who carried herself cleanly. However, he likely had no idea that I was a team leader in such a large company. This explains his disrespectful behavior.

In American companies, sexual harassment and harassment are serious legal issues. When such incidents are reported to the company's HR (Human Resources) department, they initiate an investigation and conduct interviews with relevant employees. A specialized attorney may be employed to determine the facts, and appropriate actions, including termination and disciplinary measures, are taken based on the findings.

At that time, I was a divorced single woman. Not to boast, but I had a slim figure and long hair that I spent a good forty-five minutes each day styling with a hair dryer. I wanted to look clean and well-kept, possibly because I grew up in South Korea, where, among my two sisters, I was never considered the "pretty" one.

Instead of hearing compliments about my looks, I was called "flat face," a term that referred to my low nose bridge. My nose was low, and this complex bothered me. I didn't have double eyelids, so

I'd draw eyeliner in the morning, and by evening, it would often form two lines.

My nose was flat, my eyes were small, and my upper eyelid crease lacks the prominence of a Caucasian eye's crease, resulting in a slit like appearance. I even underwent double eyelid surgery in South Korea for a more appealing look and for the medical reason that my eyelid kept hitting on my eyeballs.

Even now, when I look in the mirror, I don't think I'm pretty. But living in the United States, I noticed something strange. Without my asking, the native Americans often commented that my low nose bridge was beautiful.

One Korean woman advised me not to smile in front of men. I've been outgoing by nature since I was a baby, and I'm good at striking up conversations with strangers.

Here's a story my mother told me: When I was just a baby, my mother had something to attend to and took me with her on a crowded bus. The bus was packed with people, and someone inadvertently pushed me out of my mother's arms. I ended up in the hands of the man standing behind me.

Man on the bus: "Oh, look at this little one. She's not crying even though a stranger is holding her. She's smiling!"

I was raised with kindness and love, and it made me a friendly person. So, when I came to the United States, I often engaged in small talk with people I didn't know. I don't feel it, but I don't understand why Korean people put such restrictions on my behavior. It must be a cultural thing.

WHY AREN'T YOU TAKING A BATH!

While serving as a team leader in that company, I once held a meeting with upper management to install a new machine for packaging finished products. I decided to take charge of training on how to use the machine and began teaching an Indian temporary worker, from India, who had just joined us. The products we were packaging were not particularly heavy, but during the training, the employee started sweating profusely since he had to pack products all day.

With the sweat came a strong odor emanating from the worker's body. It gave me a headache and made me feel nauseous. I had to keep my distance while getting through the training. Eventually, the temporary worker began working with other employees the following day.

After a few days, my colleagues who worked alongside the temporary worker started complaining to me about the unpleasant odor he emitted. I didn't want to make the worker uncomfortable, so instead of addressing him directly, I called the temporary employment manager and asked if he could kindly advise the worker to shower more often or maintain a cleaner state while working.

The worker didn't show up for work the next day, and when I called the temporary employment manager, he said: "In India, there is a period when we don't take showers, but I'll make sure he gets it sorted out."

It's known that in India, there are periods when people abstain from bathing due to religious or regional customs. The specific timing and reasons can vary depending on the region and religion.

So, I thought that the Indian temporary worker, feeling upset after our previous discussion, wouldn't return to work. However, after two days, he came back with a thoroughly clean body and a fresh scent. He worked very diligently afterward and was eventually hired as a full-time employee.

A few years ago, when I visited Jeju Island in Korea, I encountered an Indian passenger seated in the front row of a plane, and I remembered the unpleasant odor due to religious reasons and that specific period. Understanding these cultural and religious practices made it easier for me to tolerate the smell and exercise patience.

Additionally, I am grateful to God for creating us in such a way that, after smelling something for a while, we become desensitized to it, preventing us from being repelled by unpleasant odors.

As a Christian, I appreciate the freedom to shower whenever I want, as there are no restrictions on hygiene practices.

I read an article in Christian Today. Open Doors released its annual report in 2021, known as the World Watch List (WWL), which ranks the top fifty countries where Christians, who believe in Christ, face severe persecution. The report revealed that one in every eight Christians worldwide is persecuted, with two out of five Christians in Asia and one out of six Christians in Africa facing persecution.

According to the Open Doors report for the period from 2019 to 2020, here are the top ten countries with the most severe persecution of Christians and the top ten countries where Christians face the most severe violence:

Top Ten Countries with Most Severe Persecution of Christians:

North Korea

Afghanistan

Somalia

Libya

Pakistan

Eritrea

Yemen

Iran

Nigeria

India

Top Ten Countries with Most Severe Violence against Christians:

Pakistan

Nigeria

Democratic Republic of the Congo

Mozambique

Cameroon

Central African Republic

India

Mali

South Sudan

Ethiopia

It's a reminder of how fortunate we are to believe in Jesus, live in countries like South Korea or the United States where we don't face persecution, and have the freedom to practice our faith and shower as we please. When Christians in persecuted countries see how we live, they may consider it a glimpse of heaven.

> Before ascending to heaven, Jesus spoke to his disciples, saying, "But you will receive power when the Holy Spirit has come upon you, and you will be my witnesses in Jerusalem and in all Judea and Samaria, and to the end of the earth" (Acts 1:8 ESV).

One day, I hope that we can be witnesses for Jesus to the ends of the earth and share the gospel with those who have not yet heard.

CORPORATE SEPARATION

I spent several years enjoying my job and creating IBM products with enthusiasm. One day, the company announced that due to an overwhelming number of orders, the production and shipping departments would be moving to a larger building about five minutes away from the headquarters. After the relocation was completed, I officially began managing the department.

The new building was approximately five times larger than the old one. With this expansion came increased production, requiring more time to manage efficiently. I oversaw the transition to an automated system in the production department.

I also worked with engineers to research lean manufacturing methods, sitting at each station to manufacture products directly and reduce time and resource waste. I focused on employee training and productivity improvement.

Once the new building was set up, and production was running smoothly, one day, my manager approached me and said, "Jennifer, the company is expanding, and we're hiring more employees. We need to be prepared for continued growth."

I replied, "Yes, that's right."

The manager continued, "So, as part of the preparation process, we're considering promoting you to a supervisory role. How do you feel about that?"

I said, "Thank you. But I hope the change to a salaried position doesn't lead to a reduction in pay. I often work overtime, and I'm concerned that switching to a monthly salary might decrease my earnings."

A while later, while discussing this potential promotion with another supervisor candidate, we headed out for lunch with our manager. During the car ride, my manager handed me a document: my future salary statement, which included a higher amount, considering the overtime I worked.

As a result, I decided to accept the supervisory role and began overseeing both the morning and evening shifts, managing a team of six team leaders and approximately one hundred employees.

There was a Korean man from the shipping department who attended the morning meetings with us every day. I assisted him in making the reports he brought to the meetings even more detailed and well-organized, teaching him how to present essential information to the managers effectively. Since then, the managers always thanked this Korean colleague after the meetings, which led to improved performance reviews and increased pay on the quarterly performance reports. He even made a lighthearted comment to me at one point.

Shipping and Korean colleague: "Thank you for always helping me. But, Jennifer, you're like a Korean on the outside, but your thoughts seem American."

I replied, "I can't quite feel it, but if you say so."

One busy workday, I received a call from my younger sister in Korea, who was very upset. She explained that our mother, who was undergoing medical treatment in Korea, had a severe nosebleed at the hospital and might not make it. She cried inconsolably.

She had called me before when our mother was hospitalized for liver cancer and asked me to come to Korea, but I couldn't go due to work commitments. At that time, I told her that I couldn't go because of a heavy workload and various responsibilities, including the relocation of the production department to a new building.

However, this time, hearing my younger sister's distress over the phone, I couldn't hold back my tears, and I wept at my desk. Tears welled up and mascara ran down my face. Unable to stop crying, I went to my manager's desk, told them about my mother's condition, and explained that I needed to leave for Korea the next day to see her.

My manager understood the situation, and the next day, I purchased a plane ticket to Korea. I arrived in Korea and went to the hospital where my mother was admitted. She was overjoyed to see me and said that she wanted to come back to the United States and live with me once she recovered.

At that time, I didn't know the extent of my mother's illness, but I replied to her with a hopeful heart.

CHAPTER 9

Fight with Liver Cancer

Chapter 9 is based on the diary my sister wrote about our mother's hospital stay, which I edited. As my sister stood unwavering by my mother's side during those challenging months in the hospital, she diligently penned the pages of her diary, capturing not just the passing days but the intricate moments that stitched together the fabric of their shared journey. The whispered exchanges that only a daughter and mother could understand, the diary became a vessel for emotions, a testament to resilience.
And then, as the final moments approached, the diary's ink seemed to hold the essence of those bittersweet farewells.
It wasn't just a record; it became memories etched with the tenderness of a daughter bidding farewell to her beloved mother. Thus, her story unfolds, a testament to the enduring strength of love and the power of bearing witness to life's most profound moments.
Here marks the beginning of her enduring care and love, as the pages of her diary unfold.

LAST THANKSGIVING

At that time, I was going through a challenging personal period and was feeling worn out from a series of tough days. After some time, I mustered the strength to visit my youngest sister's place during the Chuseok (the Korean thanksgiving) holiday to see our mom.

We gathered with other family members and enjoyed a meal together, sharing stories and briefly chatting with our mom. She told me she had severe pain without a specific location and had received acupuncture on her ribcage a few days earlier at a traditional Korean medicine clinic.

As a nurse, I couldn't understand why I hadn't thought of doing an ultrasound when she was in so much pain. Seeing her changed face and hearing her complaints of pain deeply worried me. After some time, I shared my concerns with my younger brother, telling him that I thought our mom might not make it. He didn't want to hear it and gave me a somewhat annoyed response, mentioning that our mom's condition was uncertain.

Later, I grew increasingly worried about our mom's health and went to visit her at my younger sister's place again. During our conversation, our mom suddenly handed me the gold ring I had given her, telling me to take it and that I had given it to her. She also gave me an expensive fur coat I had bought for her because she had kept insisting, she wanted to wear it, even though it was quite a financial stretch for me. She said I should take it, too.

Sometimes I used to buy clothes that she didn't like for herself, and she would immediately ask me to return them for a refund. But when I bought her clothes that she liked, she would eagerly try them on, again and again and didn't come out of her bedroom. She had a strong desire for new clothes.

Then, her unusual behavior started to worry me. She began cleaning and organizing her room meticulously. She would say things that indicated she might be feeling seriously unwell or that she believed she was going to die. Her actions became increasingly strange. I can never forget the look on her face during those times, a face that was turning an eerily dark color.

IN THE EMERGENCY ROOM

I was at work when I received a call from my youngest sister. She urgently asked me to come to the emergency room, where they had taken our mom. I quickly wrapped up my work and headed to the emergency room. When I arrived, I found my mom lying on a high hospital bed, and she was in so much pain that she was sitting up. The hospital staff couldn't find anything wrong with her on the X-ray and told us we could go home.

My mom kept complaining about the pain, and it was only then that the doctor prepared for an ultrasound. After analyzing the ultrasound results, the doctors and nurses suddenly became busy, telling us that she needed to be admitted to the hospital. When we asked for the reason, they told us that she had been diagnosed with liver cancer.

It was frustrating to go from being told she could be discharged to now needing to be admitted. We tried to find an available room for her, but the hospital was full, so she had to spend four days in the emergency room. Amidst all this, I remembered something funny my mom once said.

Mom: "You need connections for hospitals. Without connection, you die."

While my mom was stuck in the emergency room unable to secure a room, I discovered that my youngest aunt's second son-in-law, who graduated from Seoul National University's medical school, was interning at that hospital. With his help, we were able to monitor my mom's condition and eventually find a room for her to be admitted to.

ADMITTED TO THE HOSPITAL ROOM

After enduring four uncomfortable days in the emergency room, we finally moved to a regular hospital room, which turned out to be a five-person ward. Shortly after that, my mom's primary doctor called me in for a consultation.

The doctor informed me that my mom had stage four liver cancer, and her condition had severely deteriorated, with not much time left. Despite my mom looking relatively healthy on the surface, the doctor's words were incomprehensible and beyond belief.

Following that initial consultation, the doctor repeatedly informed me about my mom's diagnosis day after day, as if he believed I hadn't understood it the first time. After several repetitions, I had no choice but to tell the doctor that I was a nurse. Subsequently, the doctor stopped repeating the diagnosis.

A little while after her admission, my mom developed ascites, which accounted for 85 percent of the ascites cases, characterized by fluid accumulation in the abdominal cavity. Ascites can occur due to various reasons such as cirrhosis of the liver, congestive heart failure, malignant tumors, tuberculosis, and so on.

Ascites can be divided into two main categories: transudative ascites and exudative ascites. Transudative ascites occur when there is an increase in pressure within the blood vessels due to conditions like liver cirrhosis or congestive heart failure. It typically has a clear or straw-colored appearance and contains lower protein levels and cellular components compared to exudative ascites.

Exudative ascites may occur when there is an increase in protein-rich fluid in the abdominal cavity due to factors like infection, pancreatitis, tumors, etc. It typically appears cloudy and has a higher protein concentration compared to transudative ascites.

When ascites develops in the abdomen, the abdomen becomes distended, body weight increases, and discomfort ensues. This condition can lead to various symptoms, including loss of appetite, indigestion, and digestive problems when it exerts pressure on the stomach and intestines.

Upon draining my mom's ascites, a small amount of blood came out, whereas clear ascitic fluid should have been expected. The doctor who witnessed this shook his head in puzzlement and left the room. As my mom's condition continued to deteriorate over time, the primary doctor repeatedly prepared me for what seemed to be a potentially grim outcome.

INPATIENT DAILY JOURNAL 1

Mom was showing classic signs of liver disease due to her liver cancer. She was experiencing extreme fatigue, irritability, and a sense of heaviness and bloating in her abdomen, which added to her daily discomfort.

There was no one available to care for her in her condition, so we sought the help of a caregiver. However, my mom felt uneasy with no one else besides me. Perhaps it was because she felt less embarrassed in front of her own child, who assisted her even with the most private and sensitive tasks like helping with bowel movements and urination, due to her abdominal distension caused by the ascites.

I would leave work, provide care for my mom, sleep and eat at the hospital, then return to work. My mom had specific cravings, and she especially missed the American food she used to eat in the United States, including salads and puddings.

However, when I went to great lengths to buy these for her at a local department store, she would refuse to eat them, complaining that they weren't fresh enough or had gone bad due to being greasy.

I was exhausted from working all day, taking care of my mom, and traveling back and forth between home and the hospital. Nevertheless, my mom didn't seem to sympathize with my fatigue. During the day, she would sleep, and she would wake up at two in the morning, but she would disturb my sleep, saying things like:

Mom: "Why are you so sleepy?"
Me: "Mom, what?" . . . (yawn)

Mom: "Give me something to eat . . . Yeah, bring me some dried rice crispy."

Mom had strong teeth, and everyone marveled at how she could chew that hard dry rice cake. At exactly two in the morning, she would eat it with determination, then ask for water. It seemed like she didn't think too much about her children going through so much trouble for her, whether her symptoms were related to liver cancer or not.

INPATIENT DAILY JOURNAL 2

Mom would sleep during the day and always wake up at exactly two in the morning, disturbing my sleep. She would fuss, unable to sleep, and demand sleeping pills. Reluctantly, I revealed that I was a nurse and gave her metoclopramide (macsolong), an antacid, instead of a sleeping pill.

The next day, she announced that she had a bout of dizziness from the "sleeping pill" and would never take it again. A few days later, I had an episode of dizziness from exhaustion while using the restroom adjacent to the hospital room. I was drained from caring for Mom and working, so I found myself passed out on the bathroom floor for a few seconds.

Feeling extremely tired, I decided to take turns caring for Mom with my younger brother. Before our shift change, I quietly asked my brother to provide Mom with a fake sleeping pill if she requested it. One day, my brother completely disregarded my secret plea and discovered that the "sleeping pills" were macsolong antacid. I was really tempted to give him a piece of my mind for his insensitivity.

One time, she asked my sister-in-law to make sticky rice cakes for her, but when she tried them and found them too salty, she threw a fit and refused to eat. Mom's irritability was increasing day by day, and she began pestering her family incessantly with her demands.

One weekend, after church, my younger brother and his family visited. They didn't come to visit Mom, who was staying at a hotel during her treatment, but to visit her at the hospital. They brought baguettes and sushi, even though Mom couldn't eat those things. It seemed like they had no idea what Mom wanted to eat. Mom got irritated, saying, "Did you bring me food I can't eat?" and told them to eat the food themselves. My brother's family, apparently very hungry, devoured the food.

INPATIENT DAILY JOURNAL 3

It had been about one month and fifteen days since my mother was admitted to the hospital. I couldn't leave the hospital bed empty, so I found someone to take care of her during the day. The person I found was Elder Kwon, who used to be my son's Sunday school teacher when he was five years old.

Elder Kwon loved my son very much, and when she had a lot of pain in his legs, my young son, only five years old, would pray every day for Elder Kwon's legs not to hurt anymore. It's amazing how the power of intercessory prayer seems to be truly strong. After my son's prayers, Elder Kwon's leg pain was miraculously healed, and she said her legs no longer hurt.

> Therefore, confess your sins to each other and pray for each other so that you may be healed. The prayer of a righteous person is powerful and effective. (Jas 5:16)

> Truly I tell you, if two of you on earth agree about anything they ask for, it will be done for them by my Father in heaven. For where two or three gather in my name, there am I with them. (Matt 18:19–20)

During the day she came for about a week, but suddenly Elder Kwon mentioned that she couldn't continue caregiving. She explained that the reason was that my mother complained that she was not taking proper care of her and that she was just coming to have fun instead of caregiving.

Additionally, my mother urged me to not to waste money and make her stop coming, so I gave Elder Kwon a significant amount of extra money as caregiving fees. When she received the fee, she needed to buy a specific hanbok (Korean traditional clothing) for an inauguration ceremony. The extra money I gave her was precisely what she needed for the hanbok. Since then, my mother couldn't find caregivers she liked, and I ended up continuing the caregiving myself.

INPATIENT DAILY JOURNAL 4

At some point, my mother began to exhibit strange behavior. During the day, she would sleep, but at exactly 2 a.m., she would wake up and start saying that black spirits were surrounding her bed. She would urgently ask me to pray. This continued, and every day at 2 a.m., she claimed that evil spirits were congregating around her bed. I would get up to pray and provide her with food to help her through her difficult hospital life.

One day, God responded to my prayers and said:

God: "When your sister Jennifer from the United States comes, I will take your mother."

From that point on, I stopped praying for my mother's life and began preparing for her death. I moved her hospital bed to a well-lit spot. Due to her condition, she needed frequent drainage of her ascites, a procedure that involves removing fluid from her abdominal cavity, which is a blood serum component.

Ascites drainage made it difficult to monitor urine output. Her urine was dark and minimal due to dehydration. Severe constipation and frequent bowel movements added to her discomfort. Swollen legs and increasing ascites made it harder for her to breathe, eat, or move. She had always been slim for her life. She made a silly comment about her weight.

Mother: "I wish I could gain weight gracefully like this."

As time passed, her ascites worsened, breathing became more difficult, and she could hardly eat. She mainly sat in her bed, as it was challenging for her to do anything else.

INPATIENT DAILY JOURNAL 5

Once, my mother expressed her desire to eat dog meat, and my aunt would often cook it for her. According to my mother, her late mother, who passed away due to stomach cancer, had also expressed a desire for dog meat before her passing. My mother, with a worried expression, said that she felt like she might be about to die.

Mom: "I need to help your younger sister babysit her kids and I have a lot to do. I need to live a bit longer."

Sometimes, she would talk about the old days when she actively participated in church activities. She shared that she had prayed fervently with tears for her older sister, who had not received Jesus during her time. My aunt, her sister, passed away while still not having accepted Jesus. As her symptoms of liver cancer worsened, her pain increased, and she endured each day with powerful painkillers.

INPATIENT DAILY JOURNAL 6

One day, my sister, who lived in the United States, called, and said she was coming. She had initially been too busy to come when we had asked, but her sudden change of plans meant she was on her way.

At that moment, I remembered the word I believed God had given me, that my mother would be taken when my sister came. I started organizing the hospital room, and my mother, feeling upbeat, believed that she would be discharged when my sister arrived.

As I sorted through the clothes, a dress came out, and my mother insisted it wasn't hers. I smelled it, and it had my mother's scent. I assured her that she should wear it when she was discharged.

The night before my sister's arrival, I couldn't sleep. The fear of my mother's death overwhelmed me, and I felt my heart pounding as I pondered leaving my children. I couldn't sleep a wink that night.

My mother, lying beside me, noticed my sleeplessness and asked me why I couldn't sleep.

The next day, I went to the airport to pick up my sister, all the while with a heart full of anxiety. My mother, who was still feeling quite cheerful, didn't know what was happening.

On the bus to the hospital, my heart pounded with fear. I met my sister at the airport and took her to the hospital where my mother was admitted. It was the day God had told me:

God: "When your sister comes, I will be taking your mother."

I didn't reveal my feelings to anyone, just told everyone to go home as they were tired and to come back tomorrow.

INPATIENT DAILY JOURNAL 7

From the day my sister arrived, the malevolent spirits that had gathered every night around 2 a.m. stopped coming. Instead, from that evening onward, my mother began to mention that people were at the foot of her bed. At that moment, she was more lucid than ever, and I asked her:

"Mom, who is at the foot of the bed?"

Mom: "Your father, grandmother, and great-grandmother are standing there. They keep asking me to go with them."

Me: "Mom, those people are not really my father or grandmother; they are disguised spirits."

Mom: "They keep standing there and telling me to go."

From that point on, I started praying for the spirits with human disguises to go away. According to what people say, before one dies, dark spirits always come first. They take on the appearance of the person's closest and most beloved family members or loved ones, attempting to tempt them and bring them to hell.

My mother and I continued praying for those spirits to leave, and eventually, the other spirits fled. Only "my father" remained standing under the bed until the next morning. These spirits have knowledge of the people the person loved most during their lifetime, and they use that to tempt and lure them to hell until their final moment.

Mom looked at him and said, "You are not my husband," and she realized, saying, "You are spirits."

At that moment, he disappeared. From that point on, my mom began contemplating her sins and started to repent. For several days, she sat and lay on the bed, continuously praying and engaging in repentance.

Thinking that she would be discharged when my sister arrived, my mom began organizing her clothes. Meanwhile, I started preparing for her passage to heaven. I sent all my favorite clothes, including a red coat, home, keeping only one black coat in the hospital wardrobe.

The new juice boxes we kept under the bed to prevent anything from hiding there were sent home and to the nurses' station.

On the night my sister arrived, our family members had gone home, and my mom suddenly screamed, "Uoowhack!" That was when her liver possibly ruptured. Her blood pressure dropped, and her vitals worsened. Nurses quickly placed monitors around her.

I asked my mom, "Should I call my brother?"

And she was clearheaded, saying there was no need. So, I stayed by her side alone. She had been struggling to breathe and couldn't eat for a while, but that night, she became relatively stable, and she slept peacefully, a rare occurrence.

A little later, my daughter entered the room. Mother used to take care of when she was a baby. Now she had grown into a young adult. On that night, I told her to say her final goodbyes to her grandmother. My daughter brought her face close to her grandmother's ear, and they exchanged their last words. After the conversation, my daughter couldn't contain her sadness and started crying loudly beside her.

INPATIENT DAILY JOURNAL 8

The next day marked the last day of my mother's life in this world. When I woke up in the morning, I was anxious and fearful of my mother's impending death. My heart was pounding with uncertainty and sadness, but I couldn't show it to anyone.

The previous evening, my siblings had gone home, and they returned to the hospital room in the morning. It appears they all bathed before coming, even though they hadn't discussed it with each other.

Around ten in the morning, the associate pastor from our church came to the hospital room and asked my mom.

Pastor: "Sister, can you go to heaven?"

Mom: "No, I can't go to heaven."

In the afternoon, around five o'clock, the head pastor of our church, came to the hospital room. He prayed briefly with my mom and then asked her.

Pastor: "Sister, can you go to heaven now?"

Mom: "Yes, now I can go."

At 10 a.m., my mother had answered the pastor that she couldn't go to heaven, but when our head pastor asked the same question, she confidently replied that she could go to heaven.

My mother didn't explain the reason to me, but I'm not sure whether she spent those few hours reflecting on her faith and praying. It's possible that she had a meaningful spiritual experience during those six hours while conversing with God.

She continued to complain about her stomach pains, as she felt bloated due to the ongoing internal bleeding from her liver. The day was a Friday, and all the attending physicians had left for the weekend. In the afternoon, my mother's pain from the accumulating blood became unbearable. I, believing it was her day to go to heaven, sat quietly, but my mother was getting impatient and insisted on calling my younger sister to bring the doctor.

A young inexperienced female intern was called to remove the blood. However, what she extracted was not just blood from her stomach; it was blood gushing out from her ruptured liver. Normally, people shouldn't lose more than one liter of blood from their body, but during the procedure, almost two liters of bright red blood flowed out. During this, my mother said:

"Why am I like this? . . . I see a cross on the ceiling . . . people in white clothes are gathered in a circle, praying."

I saw my mother reaching her hand towards the ceiling, as if she were touching something in the air with her fingers. Quietly, I looked at what she was touching. It was a cross. My mother then said:

"Can't you see that cross up there? . . . People in white clothes are praying for me."

My mother had opened her spiritual eyes to the afterlife as her death approached. She continued to speak:

"Little baby angels are coming to greet me."

With over two liters of blood and bile removed, my mother was slipping into shock. All I could do was watch her dying moments. I quickly approached her and whispered into her ear:

"Mom, don't be afraid, you're going to heaven. You go first and wait for us."

Upon hearing these words, my mother held my hand tightly, even though she was in an unconscious state with her heart rate and blood pressure gradually dropping. Even after our church's end-of-life choir came and sang for about forty minutes, my mother's heart and breathing had stopped, yet her eyes remained open.

Next to my mother's bed, my youngest sister began crying loudly, calling out for her. My mother's heart, which had stopped, started beating again, and her pulse began to rise. The people singing hymns informed us that we shouldn't cry too much as her soul hadn't left yet.

They said that if we cried too much, her soul might suffer and not depart because of her grieving children. So, we asked the crying siblings to leave the room.

No matter how much we tried to close her eyes, my mother kept opening them. At the age of thirty-nine, she had suffered and struggled, raising her four children alone after losing her husband, leaving her alone and lonely. Her words were almost as if we could hear them.

Mom: "How can I leave my children, who have grown up without their father . . ." (sob).

After singing hymns for about an hour, imploring her to depart to heaven, my mother finally closed her eyes. Then a female intern came and declared her time of death, saying, "Your mother has passed away at this date, time, and day."

INPATIENT DAILY JOURNAL 9, MESSAGE FROM GOD

In the funeral home, I was grieving my mother's passing and feeling a deep sense of remorse for the things I had done wrong to her. These thoughts weighed heavily on my heart. Later, as I was using the restroom, I had a vision where I saw my mother in heaven, wearing a white dress and dancing. In this vision, God spoke to me, providing comfort.

God: "My beloved daughter, it's over now. You've done well. Your mother is at peace in heaven."

While caring for my mother, it was a taxing and challenging experience, but it was also a time of reconciliation and strengthening of our relationship. I am grateful to God for granting me the opportunity to care for my mother until the end.

CHAPTER 10

Holy Ground

* This chapter unfolds as a profound testimonial, one that I had the privilege of encountering from Esther. Her words, steeped in resilience and truth, resonate with an authenticity that only personal experience can imbue.

FIRST ENCOUNTER

"We are standing on holy ground, and I know there are angels all around. Let us praise Jesus now."

This song was Esther's favorite song. She always wished to stand on the church stage and sing this song to God. I first met Esther at the workplace where I worked when I first moved to the Seattle area. She was in her mid-forties, of petite stature, with a well-proportioned, somewhat plump figure. She always sat alone in the lunchroom, quietly having her lunch, and she had no friends.

I used to have my lunch alone as well, always quietly. I approached Esther's table one day, and we introduced ourselves. We started spending time together during breaks and lunch hours, gradually becoming friends.

At first, I thought she spoke English fluently, so we conversed in English for a while. We eventually introduced ourselves as Koreans, and that's when we started opening to each other in Korean.

As we got to know each other better, Esther often visited my home on weekends, and we cooked and shared meals, talking for hours. We became quite close, and Esther explained why she was proficient in English.

TRAGIC EVENT

She had a daughter and a son from her previous marriage back then. After her divorce, she started dating a man who treated her like a queen. He took her and the children on wonderful trips and they had a genuinely happy and blissful time together. After some time, her boyfriend began drinking heavily.

As time went by, her boyfriend's drinking escalated, and he started showing signs of controlling behavior and exhibited symptoms like obsessive-compulsive disorder. He became abusive, and their once-happy life became a living nightmare. He increased the amount of alcohol he consumed daily, and he trapped her in her own home, making it feel like a prison with constant psychological pressure.

Despite her efforts to persuade him to reduce his drinking and return to their happier life, he wouldn't change his ways and continued to abuse her. Esther made a difficult decision to leave the relationship and got her own apartment. She worked as a restaurant waitress and lived on her own.

Her ex-boyfriend repeatedly found her apartment and pressured her to come back home. She explained to him that she couldn't endure his alcoholism, physical abuse, psychological pressure, and mistreatment any longer and that she had no intention of reuniting with him, repeatedly telling him this dozens of times. However, he didn't give up.

Several months passed, and Esther finished her evening waitress job and headed back to her apartment around 10 p.m. As she got out of her car, she walked through the dimly lit spaces between the apartment buildings in the parking lot.

Her ex-boyfriend, who had been hiding in the darkness, spotted Esther and attacked her with a hatchet, relentlessly striking her head. Enraged by her refusal to comply with his demands, he savagely attacked her, shattering two-thirds of her skull with the hatchet, and then fled. Esther, lying in the deserted parking lot, with her skull in pieces and bleeding, was all alone.

In that apartment complex, there was a Korean church deacon couple who didn't know Esther. That night, the deacon couple was watching TV when they heard someone knocking on the apartment door. They were surprised to hear a knock on the door at such a late hour, with no expected visitors. Wondering if it was a mistake or if they had misheard, they decided to ignore it and continued watching TV.

After a few minutes, there was another knock at the door. This time, the deacon couple, now certain that they had heard it, wondered who could be visiting at this late hour and decided to open the door and look outside.

When they looked outside, there was no one at their doorstep. They walked towards the parking lot, thinking someone might be outside. It was late, and there were no passersby, but in the distance, they spotted a woman bleeding profusely, her head shattered and lying on the ground. They immediately called 911.

A while later, Esther's ex-boyfriend was arrested by the police and is currently serving time in prison.

The horrific nature of the incident catapulted it, gaining such prominence that it was featured on the front page of a well-known newspaper, as she recounted to me.

Esther was rushed to the emergency room in a whirlwind of urgency and concern, where she found herself on the surgery table for a grueling ten hours. The operation room, filled with the steady beeps of machines and the focused intensity of the medical team, became a battlefield for her survival. During the meticulous procedure, surgeons, under the harsh glare of surgical lights, peered through a microscope to carefully extract the shattered fragments of her skull.

They moved with a precision that was both awe-inspiring and nerve-wracking, aware that every decision carried immense weight. Despite their efforts, some extremely tiny fragments remained, embedded too deeply and precariously; attempting their removal posed a significant risk of further brain damage.

Afterward, Esther remained in a vegetative state for three months, relying on medical equipment to breathe. Doctors had given her a prognosis of a 0.001 percent chance of survival and declared her chances of recovery were virtually non-existent.

One day, three months later, Esther experienced a bright light and heard her daughter calling out, "Mom, Mom." When she opened her eyes, her daughter wasn't there, but she found herself in a hospital room.

From that point on, Esther began her recovery journey, starting with learning how to walk again. She was sent to a rehabilitation center, where she had to relearn language due to the brain damage she had suffered. Since she was in the United States, the rehabilitation center began teaching her English from the very basics, starting with the ABCs. As for how she relearned English, she didn't mention whether her memory eventually returned for speaking Korean.

I'M AN ORDINARY PERSON

After spending several months at the rehabilitation center, she gradually returned to a normal life. Esther found various jobs and eventually started working at the same place I worked. However, over half of her income had to go towards lifelong medical expenses, and her credit was so poor that she couldn't even afford a car.

She could only manage to pay rent for her apartment and make ends meet. She would drive a beaten-up car without knowing how much gas was left or how fast she was driving, often glancing at the dashboard for clues.

Esther had a calm personality, a soft-spoken voice, and a talent for singing. She felt extremely grateful to God for saving her life and wanted to sing "Holy Ground," the song mentioned earlier, on the stage of the American church to repay God's grace. She saw it as a way to give back to God.

I used to take her to American churches every Sunday, and I would request the church organizers to allow Esther to sing during special times. We managed to get her on the stage to sing at several churches. On the stage, she would sing her heart out, often moved to tears by the emotions welling up from her chest, thanking God for his grace.

At that time, I was divorced from my ex-husband and in a situation where I had to work to make a living, and I didn't have any significant assets apart from a good credit score. Her financial situation was tight, and she had issues with her car.

So, I went to a dealership and bought a car for her on my name, arranging a payment plan. The car was quite old, but it was something that could run decently. She was ecstatic driving her own car, and she promised to pay me for her car payment with small amounts of money every month.

She drove the car with immense happiness, and she was doing her best to live a normal life. After a few months had passed, she started behaving strangely, eating a lot of food she bought and fumbling around in the car. Her gaze changed a little, and I began to sense that something was going wrong with her.

And then she started to miss work repeatedly and didn't show up. A few days later, when Esther finally came to work, I approached her with a welcoming and concerned attitude. However, she opened her eyes wide and gave me a hostile, piercing look, telling me not to come near her and even using harsh language.

I kept asking her what was wrong, but she continued to shout, telling me to stay away. So, I demanded that she give me her car keys and told her I would drive her home. She cursed while slamming her car keys on the ground. I drove her home and left, telling her that I would contact her after she had rested and felt better.

I waited for several days, but I didn't receive any contact from her. I decided to visit her home, and when I got there, she was not at home. I went back again after a while, but she still wasn't there.

I then approached the apartment manager to inquire about Esther. The apartment manager informed me that a few Korean women had taken her somewhere recently, and they had canceled their apartment lease.

In the southern farm area of Seattle, there's a place with about ten acres of land, containing several houses and small buildings. It's a shelter for abused women who live in isolation, and they absolutely do not disclose their names to outsiders. I don't know if Esther is at that place or not, but I earnestly hope that she is living safely there.

In that quiet, secluded corner, where the land stretches out like a protective embrace, lies the hope of refuge for those like Esther. The thought of her possibly being there, in a place where whispered fears transform into pillars of strength, offers peace to my restless mind. The secrecy surrounding the shelter's inhabitants, a necessary veil of privacy, leaves me in a state of anxious hope. I find myself often pondering, with a heart heavy yet hopeful, wishing beyond wishes that Esther has found her way to this sanctuary.

CHAPTER 11

The Angels and Satan

DISTANT UNCLE

While writing this book, I went back and forth several times, especially with chapter 11, the distant uncle.

I initially gave it a title and placed it in the middle of the book's table of contents, but later moved it to the end. I contemplated this for a month. It felt like I was bearing my soul, revealing a sensitive and somewhat uncomfortable part of my life.

Then, I debated whether to include this chapter at the end of the book. However, I started contemplating readers who might have shared similar experiences but hesitate to open up, seeking the proper assistance or healing they deserve. I mustered the courage to write this chapter.

When I was young, my mother allowed relatives from the countryside to stay at our home temporarily, particularly when they came to Seoul for various reasons, like going to school or trying to establish themselves.

My youngest aunt and uncle stayed with us until they got married, and a couple of other cousins attended school while living at our place. Our house was a typical one with three rooms, a small restroom, a kitchen, a master bedroom, and a central living room connecting them. We also had a small front yard beyond the front gate.

This instance refers to a distant uncle who stayed with us for a while. At the time, my older sister was in the fifth grade, and I was in the second grade of elementary school. I couldn't quite understand why my mom had us share a room with him, given that we were young girls, and he was an adult male, even though he was a relative.

I believe he was in twenties or so. He demanded of my sister and I sleep to close to the edge of a wall in the room so that he could sleep in between us when we shared a room with him. I usually wake up from my sleep due to sensitivity toward slight movements and a little sound around me.

On one occasion, I felt he was touching my body slowly from the chest to my private part with his filthy fingers. I was very furious and angry about why he was doing evil things to me.

However, I didn't say anything to him and turned my body away from him. Then he stopped his action and fell asleep. He continued his sexual assault to us at deep nights for many days between my older sister and I.

If I could stop evil wicked intentions that led to the heart of the conspiracy in his head, I started to sleep on my stomach, but he continued. The school didn't have any sexual assault education program to teach us or provide any counselling. So, we didn't know anything about it, but we knew that what he was doing was wrong. And I don't know why we didn't tell our mother.

And then, twenty years later, in my early thirties, while living in the United States, the memories of the sexual assault started coming back from the back burner of a far corner of my brain. The disturbing actions of that man were vividly recalled, and I was consumed with rage. The thoughts wouldn't stop.

A burning desire for revenge ignited within me. Additionally, this caused severe psychological stress, manifesting as overwhelming anxiety that ravaged my body. Recollections of the man's vile actions brought on severe headaches, breathlessness, dry mouth, muscle tension, abdominal cramps, rapid heartbeat, and sleep disturbances. My body experienced physical symptoms of extreme anxiety.

So, I decided to visit South Korea, believing that my mother would have the man's contact information. At that time, I felt an intense urge to go to Korea and find that man to make him pay for his actions. Upon arriving in Korea, I asked my sister if she had been subjected to the same sexual harassment in that room. She confirmed that she had indeed experienced the same.

And then, I explained to my mother what happened during the incident in the room when he was staying with us, insisting that I must find him and requesting her to provide his contact information. Filled with determination and anger, my mother said she didn't know, and she made calls to various relatives, starting with her older sister, instructing them to deny any knowledge of him if I called to inquire while searching for him.

While visiting Korea, I attempted to find the man in my own way. Throughout that time, the thought of him potentially getting married and having a daughter like me haunted my mind. I searched and searched but ultimately couldn't find him, so I returned to the United States, consumed with anger.

Then, sometime later, the Holy Spirit granted me enlightenment.

Holy Spirit: "You must forgive that man . . . not for his sake but for yours."

I couldn't forgive him at all, and I didn't want to forgive him either. I uttered forgiveness for that man insincerely and falsely. I spat it out every time anger welled up within me. Gradually, at some point, it began to take root. It became forgiveness. And I began to repent and pray for him.

Jennifer: "God, I am the worst of sinners. I have committed great sins in thought. Forgive me. I was filled with so much anger towards him that I wanted to kill him in my thoughts. Forgive this sinner. I don't know whether that man got married and had daughters, but please prevent him from doing such terrible things to his own children or any other girls. Lead him to repent for his sins and come to God. And I forgive that man."

Now, I don't hate that man because I have forgiven him. I don't want to remember, but if any circumstances force me to recall, I simply let it flow away to a distant corner of my memory.

I visited Korea twenty-four hours before my mother passed away. My mother passed, had been admitted to the hospital, and had spent the last three days in an underground area for her funeral rites. During these three days, our immediate family, my mother's siblings, aunts, and uncles came to pay their respects. On the third day, more distant relatives arrived to show their respects.

During the three days, there were a few small tables for visitors in the room. I saw my uncle asked me to come over to meet some of our distant relatives. When I went to the table one man took my right hand and spoke.

Distant uncle: "You're the one, that girl, who has grown up a lot."

The moment he held my hand, I was telling in my thought:

"I know who you are. And you are the person who sexually assaulted me and my older sister before."

As he held my hand, my mind raced, and I felt his touch filthy. I quickly withdrew my hand from his grip and left the spot. Although I spoke to him in my mind, I didn't harbor hatred towards him. When I returned to the United States and remembered the moment he held my hand during my mother's funeral, dark thoughts came into my mind.

Satan: "Why didn't you grab that man by the hair, beat him, and kick him? Why didn't you expose his deeds loudly in front of everyone to shame him and make him unable to show his face to the world? Isn't that what you should have done?"

I responded to the Satan, saying:

"Satan! In the name of our Lord Jesus Christ, be silent and depart! I have already forgiven that man!"

After that, the Satan no longer inserted thoughts of seeking revenge against that man into my mind. I recalled the words of the apostle Paul in Gal 5:16–17:

> "I say then: Walk in the Spirit, and you shall not fulfill the lust of the flesh. For the flesh lusts against the Spirit, and the Spirit against the flesh; and these are contrary to one another so that you do not do the things that you wish."

And furthermore, in verses 18–24, where it talks about how those who belong to Christ have crucified the flesh with its passions and desires:

> But if you are led by the Spirit, you are not under the law. Now the works of the flesh are evident, which are: adultery, fornication, uncleanness, lewdness, idolatry, sorcery, hatred, contentions, jealousies, outbursts of wrath, selfish ambitions, dissensions, heresies, envy, murders, drunkenness, revelries, and the like; of which I tell you beforehand, just as I also told you in time past, that those who practice such things will not inherit the kingdom of God. But the fruit of the Spirit is love, joy, peace, longsuffering, kindness, goodness, faithfulness, gentleness, self-control. Against such there is no law. And those who are Christ's have crucified the flesh with its passions and desires.

I don't know if that man accepted Jesus or not. However, I wonder if he believed in Jesus and engraved these verses in his heart, could he have acted that way?

I am truly thankful that Jesus taught us how to forgive and receive forgiveness. It is a powerful tool to stand against the Satan.

> If you forgive others their trespasses, your heavenly Father will also forgive you. (Matt 6:14)

> Bearing with one another and, if one has a complaint against another, forgiving each other; as the Lord has forgiven you, so you also must forgive. (Col 3:13)

> And whenever you stand praying, forgive, if you have anything against anyone, so that your Father also who is in heaven may forgive you your trespasses. (Mark 11:25)

> Therefore, submit to God. Resist the devil, and he will flee from you. (Jas 4:7)

Satan was originally an angel, a unique being with spiritual qualities. He knows everything about us, our likes, and dislikes, and always knows how to tempt us when an opportunity arises.

Using these tactics, he constantly roams to and searches like a roaring lion, seeking whom he may devour and testing them with all sorts of temptations. Even Jesus himself was tested by Satan for forty days in the wilderness when he was hungry after fasting.

So, we must stand firm in faith and resist the devil. When thoughts come into our minds, we should discern whether they are of the devil or not, read the Bible, pray, and seek the guidance of the Holy Spirit. We need to strengthen our faith to resist these temptations from the evil one.

GUIDING ANGELS

This time, I will write about my experiences with the protection of angels throughout my life.

First, this happened when I was in college. After entering college, I joined the mountain climbing club and practiced climbing in Mount Bukhan National Park on weekends. One weekend morning, we decided to go to an area near Podeung Ridge for basic climbing practice, surrounded by rocks.

We were told it was a good place for basic climbing practice and I followed the senior club members. As a new member of the mountain climbing club, we were a group of around six, including both males and females.

I waited for my turn in the queue. One senior secured the rope at the top and attached a carabiner, but I decided to descend and climb back up a short distance of the cliff without using any safety gear.

When I was about halfway down, I lost my balance and hung upside down on the rope. If I had fallen, there were no trees around, and I would have plummeted straight onto the rocks below. For some reason, my right ankle got entangled with the rope and saved me from falling.

One senior quickly descended on another rope to rescue me. At that moment, I could have fallen due to losing my balance, but some force caused my ankle to get caught in the rope, preventing me from falling onto the rocks.

Secondly, this incident happened when I was living in Colorado. One Friday, my husband and I had been out with friends until around 2 a.m. and were driving on a small highway with a seemingly endless view of cornfields. We were very tired and the only car on the road.

As we approached a green traffic light about one hundred meters ahead, with no other cars around at that early hour, our car continued to drive without stopping at the signal. Just as we were getting close to the light, seemingly out of nowhere, a semi-truck with six wheels appeared, making a left turn.

In that split second, my husband and I simultaneously slammed on the brakes and yelled out in fear. We thought for sure that our car was going to crash into the middle of the truck. In that moment, we felt an incredible force pushing our car backward, as if by some unknown power, and our car came to a stop just before the front of the truck making the left turn an inch away front of our eyes.

Thirdly, while living in Colorado during the Christmas season, I was visiting my mother-in-law's house and returning to Colorado. When driving long distances on the highway, it's common to find yourself unintentionally in a group of cars all heading in the same direction.

We were driving together as part of this group on the highway, but then we saw a sign indicating the next rest area was ahead, so we decided to exit the highway as the rest area would be a good place to take a break, stretch our legs, and attend to our dog.

Our dog, who usually relieves herself quickly, began circling and barking, seemingly with no way to do her business. After trying to encourage her for about ten minutes, we gave up, got in the car, and re-entered the highway.

After about five minutes of driving, we encountered a scene where a heavy snowfall had occurred. Up ahead, a police car was approaching, and we realized that an accident had occurred just minutes ago.

Looking at the cars, we saw that the vehicles from the group we had been driving with earlier had all flipped over into the ditches on both sides of the road. My husband and I looked at each other and, in disbelief, thanked our dog for delaying us as her behavior likely saved our lives.

Fourthly, on a morning when Colorado received its first heavy snowfall after moving there, I experienced a challenging commute. I had no experience driving on snowy roads, and the conditions were extremely slippery. There was a small white truck ahead of me on my way to work.

When the traffic light turned red, the cars in front of me came to a stop. I applied the brakes suddenly, but my car started to skid forward on the slippery, snow-covered road, which was a terrifying experience. In my mind, I thought:

"I'm going to rear-end the car in front of me! I'm going to hit them!"

And just then, my car changed direction and veered to the right, narrowly avoiding the other vehicle by just an inch, and ended up in a ditch.

Looking around, I noticed that the residents in the well-prepared area of the road, who were used to driving in such conditions, had no accidents except for my car. I abandoned my car in the ditch and walked home, shouldering a snow shovel, and my husband and I embarked on a mission to rescue the stranded vehicle.

Fifthly, on a day when I was driving to visit a friend's house in Seattle, I was on the highway. I was traveling on a four-lane highway, with two lanes going southbound. There was a truck carrying a mattress in the right lane, and they hadn't properly secured it with safety straps.

I felt uneasy about the situation and wanted to pass the truck. I attempted to change lanes to the left, but the heavy flow of traffic from behind made it difficult. I kept looking at the gap in the left lane while keeping an eye on the mattress truck.

Suddenly, an opportunity presented itself. In the span of just one second, I changed lanes, and at that exact moment, the mattress that was on the truck flew off and landed behind it. I looked in my rearview mirror and saw that the mattress had bounced once on the road and then landed in a ditch.

The driver of the car behind me extended their arm out of the window and gave me a thumbs-up sign, acknowledging the close call.

Now, this time I have a testimony from two American men in Seattle.

First, a middle-aged American man living in the United States shared a story. He explained that he had been going through a rough patch in his marriage, with several arguments and difficult times with his wife.

One day, he left work early and entered their bedroom at home. He was shocked to find his wife engaged in an illicit affair with another man in their bed. This discovery led to intense arguments and, eventually, his wife left him.

Overwhelmed by the situation and falling into depression, he lost his will to live. Alone in the house one day, he contemplated ending his life by pointing a small handgun he owned at his head and pulling the trigger.

At that very moment when he was about to end it all, with no one else around, he felt someone gently lowering the gun away from his head. He was absolutely certain it was an angel. He then placed the gun on the floor and wept, praying fervently to God with tears streaming down his face.

Secondly, an American man in his mid-thirties shared a remarkable experience. He took his small boat to a lake one day for a fishing trip, accompanied by his son. While they were in the middle of the lake, something like mist descended from the sky, and in the form of an angel, his best friend was smiling down at him from the air.

He found this extraordinary and somewhat unbelievable. After they finished fishing and returned home, his wife received a phone call that informed them of their best friend's passing. He immediately called his friend's house to inquire about the time of his passing. It turned out that the time he saw his friend in the angelic form from his boat matched precisely with the same time of his friend's death.

These testimonies are actual events that happened to me and others. Moreover, the Bible contains verses indicating that God sends his angels to protect us:

> He will command his angels concerning you to guard you in all your ways. (Ps 91:11)
>
> The angel of the Lord encamps around those who fear him, and he delivers them. (Ps 34:7)
>
> Are they not all ministering spirits sent out to serve for the sake of those who are to inherit salvation? (Heb 1:14)
>
> Behold, I send an angel before you to guard you on the way and to bring you to the place that I have prepared. (Exod 23:20)
>
> See that you do not despise one of these little ones. For I tell you that in heaven, their angels always see the face of my Father who is in heaven. (Matt 18:10)

By believing in the triune God—God the Father, Jesus Christ, and the Holy Spirit—I know that God sends his angels to watch over me on all my paths. I am so thankful and lost for words to express my gratitude to God, my Father, who surrounds and protects me.

The more I get to know God, the stronger I become, yet I also realize my own insignificance. My Father, the One who heals me and makes me strong, is God. Isaiah 41:10 encourages us not to fear because God is with us.

God makes me strong and truly assists me. He holds me with his righteous right hand. We are, indeed, I am the precious and noble children of God. Like the apple of his eye, his daughters, and sons. We love you God and thank you. May all the glory of the world be yours alone. Hallelujah, Amen.

www.ingramcontent.com/pod-product-compliance
Lightning Source LLC
Chambersburg PA
CBHW070454090426